12-5-63 /

EASTON

SEP 1 1982 PINEDALE

NOV 1 3 1963

394.9   Hadfield, Miles
H11   The twelve days of Christmas. Little,
            1961.
            176p. illus. 7.50

Copy 10

1. Christmas. I. Title.

11

THE
TWELVE DAYS
OF
CHRISTMAS

The first Christmas card. Designed by J. C. Horsley, 1843. *Victoria and Albert Museum.*

The Adoration of the Shepherds. Detail of stained glass window at East Harling, Norfolk. Fifteenth century. Photograph by Birkin Haward, A.R.I.B.A.

MILES & JOHN HADFIELD

THE
TWELVE DAYS
OF
CHRISTMAS

LITTLE, BROWN AND COMPANY
Boston   Toronto

LIBRARY OF CONGRESS CATALOG CARD NO. 62–18128

FIRST AMERICAN EDITION

Printed in Great Britain

Introduction

'The twelve days from Christmas to Epiphany . . . appear to be an ancient intercalary period equating the lunar to the solar year.' So wrote a learned authority a year or two ago. In his great *Dictionary of the English Language*, published two centuries earlier, Dr Johnson defined Christmas as 'the day on which the nativity of our blessed Saviour is celebrated, by the particular service of the church'.

Between the vast, archaic implications of the former statement and the limited yet more pregnant terms of the latter definition lies an immense territory of the human mind and spirit. Any exploration of it must lead through wildernesses of primeval science, magic and mysticism.

If one also considers that in the northern hemisphere the Christmas period immediately succeeds the winter solstice, when the sun is observably regaining strength and once again initiating the cycle of life and fertility, it is not surprising that within these twelve days, even in a largely materialistic world, there still remains a profound significance.

The spiritual element of Christmas still inspires, and is enhanced by, all branches of the Christian faith. The more mundane element is still expressed by the simple traditions of good friendship, good feeding, and good drinking. It is not altogether fanciful to detect the pagan element in the vulgar exploitation and commercialization of Christmas, which is regularly deplored by purists and prigs, but which, after all, is a relatively innocuous manifestation of modern civilization.

Without delving deeply into the origins and ancient practices or the deep spiritual significance of the Christmas period we have sought to assemble in this book a sort of literary museum of the traditions and observances relating to the significant days which the Christian church took over from the pagans.

INTRODUCTION

At a very early stage of our investigations we decided that it would be wrong to confine ourselves to the two or three days of the Christmas holiday as now generally understood. This would mean omitting New Year's Day and Twelfth Night which are really integral parts of the Christmas season.

The isolation of two or, at the most, three days from Christmastide is a relatively recent phenomenon. Even in the last century Leigh Hunt was by no means alone in considering the great day of the holiday to be its last—Twelfth Night. Typical, too, was the entry in John Evelyn's diary for 2 January 1646: 'I want . . . to keep the rest of Christmas at my brother R. Evelyn's at Woodcote.' Today the old singing game, 'The Twelve Days of Christmas', treated as a carol, is about all that keeps the phrase alive.

We have extended the period of our survey to include Christmas Eve (though this is, strictly speaking, no part of the feast), Christmas Day itself, and the following Twelve Days which were once so significant in the pattern of the year.

The origins of Christmas are so diverse and its celebration occurs in so many countries that some of the customs (for example, 'wassailing') are celebrated on different days in different parts of the world. In England alone they may be celebrated on different days in different counties. For practical purposes we have grouped such customs together on what seems the most usual day.

Our main aim has been to give a short historical survey of the customs and traditions of each of the important days among the twelve, illustrated from contemporary sources. Our quotations are printed as nearly as possible in their original form and spelling—without which many lose their true quality. For this reason, not many very early quotations have been made: they would be almost meaningless except to scholars, and often become prosaic when modernized.

We have not included much that is of purely antiquarian or doctrinal interest; we have rather taken Christmas as we find it today, and discussed or illustrated those traditions or observances which seem recognizably connected with it.

There are many attitudes to Christmas—as will be evident from the chapter entitled 'Christmas Remembered'. Like all other expressions of fundamental experience and need, Christmas is what you make it. For our part we readily accept the view of that founder-member of the Christmas cult, Washington Irving, when he wrote:

> He who can turn churlishly away from contemplating the felicity of his fellow-beings, and sits down darkling and repining in his loneliness when all around is joyful, may have his moments of strong excitement and selfish gratification, but he wants the genial social sympathies which constitute the charm of a merry Christmas.

But the rich seasonal fare of Christmas is better digested with the aid of an occasional dose of *Sod. bicarb.* or Alka Seltzer. We therefore find room for some ironic comments and dissenting voices.

We have not glossed over the commercial exploitation of the season, with its distorted, sentimentalized evocations of the past. That aspect appeals quite genuinely to a large proportion of mankind—which is prepared to cash-up accordingly. We must beware of priggishness when we permit ourselves to smile. We have not taken up a Superior Person's view of Christmas. Robins, Good King Wenceslas and the like, which, a few decades ago, were condemned as 'bogus', are as vital a part of Christmas as more ancient rites—indeed, often more so. We might remark at this point that the Robin Redbreast and Jenny the Wren decorating old-fashioned Christmas cards and derided by the sophisticates are now seen to have intimate connexions with prehistoric rites.

This, then, is the literary basis of our book. But Christmastide has always been above all the season of visual delights, of colour and joyful ornament, of the playing of games and the acting of plays, of dressing up in gay clothes, of winter exercises, pantomimes, and parties. To match and adorn our text, therefore, we have sought pictures ranging from the sublime to the anecdotal.

We hope that the result of our activities will resemble a symbolic Christmas tree; ablaze with candles to illuminate the season and its story; hung with gifts, some of them well known and expected, others unusual; and festooned with ephemeral tinsel to sparkle against the sombre green of the traditional tree.

Acknowledgements

For permission to quote extracts from the copyright works listed below, the authors are indebted to the following:

Miss Margaret Allonby for 'A Book for Christmas' from *A Book of South African Verse*, ed. Guy Butler (Oxford University Press).

Edward Arnold Ltd for *Memoirs of Mistral*, trans. E. C. Maude.

Brandt & Brandt for *The Short Stories of Saki*.

The British Broadcasting Corporation for a broadcast description of the Christmas truce in France, 1914.

The Macmillan Company for *Kilvert's Diary*, ed. Plomer; and 'The Oxen' and 'New Year's Eve' from Thomas Hardy's *Collected Poems* (Copyright 1925 by the Macmillan Company).

The Clarendon Press for *The Diaries of John Evelyn*, ed. de Beer.

Constable & Co Ltd for 'New Year' by Helen Waddell from *Medieval Latin Lyrics*.

Curtis Brown Ltd for *Elizabeth and her German Garden* by Countess Russell.

J. M. Dent & Sons Ltd for 'Christmas Rose' from Gerald Bullett's *Collected Poems*.

Random House Inc. for 'The Flight into Egypt' by W. H. Auden from *For the Time Being* (Copyright 1944 by W. H. Auden). Reprinted from *The Collected Poetry of W. H. Auden*.

The estate of Christopher Morley for an article which appeared in *Mince Pie*.

Oxford University Press for *The Diary of a Country Parson* by J. Woodforde, ed. J. Beresford.

Routledge & Kegan Paul Ltd for 'In the Workhouse, Christmas Day' by G. R. Sims from *The Dagonet and Other Poems*.

Farrar, Straus & Cudahy for 'Carol' by W. R. Rodgers from *Europa and the Bull*.

The Times Publishing Co Ltd for 'Old and New in Italy's Christmas Cribs' (Copyright The Times Publishing Co Ltd, 1961. All rights reserved).

Mr Laurence Whistler for 'The Kissing Bough'.

New Directions for *Quite Early One Morning* by Dylan Thomas (Copyright 1954 by New Directions).

Harcourt, Brace & World, Inc. for *Lord Weary's Castle* (Copyright 1944, 1946 by Robert Lowell); and 'The Journey of the Magi' from T. S. Eliot's *Collected Poems*.

E. P. Dutton & Co., Inc. and Everyman's Library for *Diary of a Nobody* by G. and W. Grossmith; and 'Christmas Ghosts' from *The Christmas Companion* by Harry Price.

Contents

List of Illustrations

LIST OF ILLUSTRATIONS

LIST OF ILLUSTRATIONS

✦✦✦✦✦✦✦✦✦✦✦✦✦✦✦✦✦✦✦✦✦✦✦✦✦✦✦✦✦✦✦✦✦✦✦

The engravings in the text, except where otherwise stated, are by George Cruikshank. The illustrations facing pages 15, 37, 53, 84, 93, 132, 141, 144, and 145 are reproduced from prints in the Radio Times Hulton Picture Library.

1

From Saturn to Scrooge

Looking at early paintings it is delightful to observe the variety of scene and season in which the Nativity occurred. Those of us who are northern dwellers have, from the circumstances of its reiterated celebration, come to regard the occasion as a wintry one. The announcing angels appear in a star-bright wintry sky to shepherds crouching under frozen hedges; later, the Magi make their journey through the rigours of cold. For us, the setting is Milton's:

> It was the Winter wilde,
> While the Heav'n-born-childe,
>   All meanly wrapt in the rude manger lies;
> Nature in aw to him
> Hath doff'd her gawdy trim,
>   With her great Master so to sympathize:
> It was no season then for her
> To wanton with the Sun her lusty Paramour.

Medieval artists, with their more fertile imaginations, as often as not set their scene in spring (or early summer), with white sheep in green pastures under clear blue skies.

The historical circumstances of the Nativity and its celebration in early times are subjects upon which, during nineteen centuries, much has been written that is conjectural and fanciful, less (but still plenty) that is scholarly and factual. It seems reasonable to take the view that the early Church, wishing to commemorate the birth of a Saviour and a new faith, turned to those pagan festivities of ancient origin connected with the passing of the winter solstice, and moulded them to new service.

There was a suitable festival ready to the hands of the Roman fathers of the Christian Church—the Saturnalia. Saturn and his wife Ops were amongst the oldest deities of ancient Italy. Saturn, the god of agriculture, is said to have had an altar at the foot of the Capitol before Rome was founded. One account has it that when he was deposed from his throne by Jupiter he wandered to Italy, where he ruled as king in the Golden Age. In Rome he was welcomed by another ancient god, Janus (who lends his name to the month of January), and settled at the foot of the Capitol.

Eventually Saturn vanished from the earth, leaving behind him a reputation for cleverness and for devouring his sons on birth to fulfil a pledge that he would not produce a male heir. A temple was built in his honour, where his image stood, tethered by woollen bands around the feet to prevent the deity's departure.

Subsequently the Saturnalia, the great festival in his honour, was celebrated on the nineteenth, and, after Caesar's reform of the calendar, on the seventeenth, of December. Later Augustus decreed that the seventeenth should be sacred to Saturn and the nineteenth to Ops. Henceforward it appears that the seventeenth and eighteenth were devoted to the Saturnalia, and the two following days to the Opalia, a festival of Ops. Caligula added a fifth day, 'the day of youth', devoted to sports of the young. But in popular usage the festival lasted seven days.

The season was one of general joy and mirth. The woollen fetters were taken from the image of Saturn, and each man offered a pig as sacrifice. During the festival schools were closed, no war was declared or battle fought, no punishment was inflicted. In place of the toga an undress garment was worn. Distinctions of rank were laid aside: slaves sat at table with their masters or were actually waited upon by them— a reversal of rôles which later had its parallel in Christmas festivities. Gambling with dice, at other times prohibited, was now permitted and practised. All classes exchanged gifts, the commonest being wax tapers and dolls. These dolls were especially given to children, and the makers of them held a regular fair at this time.

It may be conjectured that the Saturnalia was originally a celebration of the winter solstice. Hence the legend that it was instituted by Romulus under the name of the Brumalia (*bruma* means winter solstice). The prominence given to candles at the festival points to the custom of making a new fire at this season of the year.

El Greco (1541–1614). The Adoration of the Shepherds. Detail of
the painting in the *Royal Palace, Bucharest.*

Jacob Jordaens (1593–1678). The Bean King. Detail of the painting
in the *Alte Pinakothek, Munich.*

Here we have a festival with many of the ingredients of our present Christmas, inherited in turn from the dim ages of antiquity, and ready to be adapted by the early Christians to their new transcendent faith.

Another Roman festival, the *Kalendae* of the New Year, followed soon after the Saturnalia. That this also became involved in the origins of Christmas is apparent from the Christmas *Calendas* in Provence, where a log burns from Christmas Eve until the evening of New Year's Day.

From the north came the festival Yule, lending its name to the Scandinavian celebration. The word is found in Old English and Teutonic, but its ultimate origin is obscure.

The name Christmas—and the Dutch *Kerstmisse*—are self-explanatory and comparatively modern; nor is there any great mystery in the German *Weihnacht* (sacred night) and its forms. The French *Noël*, Italian *Natale*, Welsh *Nadolig*, and Gaelic *Nollag* may all be related and of pre-Christian origin connected with the birth of the new year.

Many naïvely ingenious suggestions have been put forward for the selection of 25 December for the festival. One is based on the tradition that Christ's Passion occurred on 25 March. The same date was chosen for His conception, so that the years of His life might be complete. Go forward nine months, and we come to 25 December as His birthday.

One school of early chronologists, by means of obscurely fantastic calculations based on the Scriptures, fixed the birthday to coincide with the day of celebration of the vernal equinox, also 25 March, in the Julian calendar. This reasoning connected the Incarnation with the Creation. Later, when the Incarnation came to be viewed as beginning at the conception instead of the birth, the birth would automatically be placed nine months later.

More probably the choice of 25 December had some connexion with the feast of the Sun God on the day of the winter solstice—25 December in the Julian calendar. With the Sun God was identified Mithras, that most powerful of Persian gods, who in the centuries immediately following the birth of Christ was adopted officially by the Romans, and whose cult came near to eclipsing Christianity. It seems that the early Christians fought a battle for possession of his day—and won.

We may leave these conjectures and disputations to our modern Wise

Men—though first it would be well to recall an alteration in the calendar that has taken place. Piecemeal, country by country, over a spell of two centuries, the Julian calendar was replaced by the Gregorian system. The result is that the original Christmas Day was what is now 6 January.

It seems that the first celebration of the feast of the Nativity took place in Rome about—or just before—the year 350. The vitality of the early Christian faith was such that it dominated and took under its wing many pagan rites which we now regard as essentially Christian characteristics of the Twelve Days of Christmas—the giving of presents, the lighting of fires and candles, the decoration of houses with ever-green and berried branches, the topsy-turveydom of masters waiting upon servants and the frolics of the Lord of Misrule, the suspension of enmity, and the proclamation of peace.

The message of peace and goodwill—and hope of salvation for mankind—had already been expressed by Virgil some forty years before the Nativity (this translation is Dryden's):

> The last great Age, foretold by sacred Rimes,
> Renews its finish'd course: Saturnian times
> Roll round again; and mighty years, begun
> From their first Orb, in radiant Circles run.
> The base degenerate iron Offspring ends;
> A golden Progeny from Heaven descends.
> O chaste Lucina! speed the Mother's pains,
> And haste the glorious Birth! thy own Apollo reigns!
> The lovely Boy, with his auspicious face,
> Shall Pollio's consulship and triumph grace.
> Majestick months set out with him to their appointed Race.
> The Father banish'd virtue shall restore,
> And crimes shall threat the guilty World no more.
> The Son shall lead the life of Gods, and be
> By Gods and Heroes seen, and Gods and Heroes see.
> The jarring Nations he in peace shall bind,
> And with paternal Virtues rule Mankind.
> Unbidden Earth shall wreathing Ivy bring
> And fragrant Herbs (the promises of Spring)
> As her first offerings to her infant King.

The close and complex interweaving of pagan and Christian traditions was well described by Sir Arthur Evans after he had spent Christmas in a small town above the Adriatic, in what was then the Black Mountain—Montenegro. The elaborate celebration of the Christian occasion was grafted on to an earlier cult of ancestor worship and, he pointed out, some of the customs were surprisingly similar to those of the English described in Herrick's poems in the seventeenth century.

The Saturnalian custom of reversal of ranks—of the master waiting on his slave, and so on—survived in the Feast of Fools, the Boy Bishops, and, until Tudor times, in the Lords of Misrule. It was, however, by its nature not a custom of the common people, and so had not enough popular support to survive the attacks of the Puritans, who considered the custom obnoxiously pagan. Perhaps, however, a hint of it was carried on into the pantomime, whose theme is so often that of the poor boy or the underling finally triumphant over malevolent superiors. It possibly continued also in the hunting and killing of the wren, the King of Birds, who was for one day deposed.

Fire, in the form of Christmas candles and the tradition, if today not the fact, of the Yule log from the north is still with us.

The entertainment of friends at the Saturnalia lives on with virility in the Christmas party, though strangely the ancient habit of entertainment at the end of the Twelve Days, which continued into the nineteenth century, has almost died out—as has much else connected with Epiphany—except in the Eastern church, where it still holds an important place.

*   *   *

The Roman practice of celebrating Christmas on 25 December as a festival of the Nativity alone spread gradually throughout the Churches. In about 380 it was adopted at Constantinople. The Armenian Church, however, still does not acknowledge it. In 567 the Council of Tours declared the Twelve Days, from Christmas to Epiphany, a festal tide. In Germany Christmas was established in 813, and in Norway by King Hakon the Good in the middle of the tenth century.

To England, Sir E. K. Chambers tells us, 'Christmas came, if not with the Keltic Church, at least with St Augustine in 592. On Christmas Day, 598, more than ten thousand English converts were baptised, and by the time of Bede (who died in 734) Christmas was established, with Epiphany and Easter, as one of the three leading festivals of the year. The *Laws* of Ethelred (991–1016) and of Edward the Confessor ordained it a holy tide of peace and concord.' As elsewhere, there was soon a shift to the Christmas feast of 'Germano-Keltic' pagan folk customs, disapproved by the Church, which had formerly been celebrated on the adjacent days on either side of it.

In medieval times the most notable development of the religious aspects of the Church ceremonial took place in the country of its origin, Italy. Most important was the introduction of the *presèpio*; in English, the crib; in France, *crèche*; in Germany, *Krippe*. Its origin is attributed to St Francis of Assisi in 1224. The circumstances were recorded by St Bonaventura in his life of the Saint:

> Now three years before his death it befell that he was minded, at the town of Greccio, to celebrate the memory of the Birth of the Child Jesus, with all the added solemnity that he might, for the kindling of devotion. That this might not seem an innovation, he sought and obtained licence from the Supreme Pontiff, and then made ready a manger, and bade hay, together with an ox and an ass, be brought unto the place. The Brethren were called together, the folk assembled, the wood echoed with their voices, and that august night was made radiant with many bright lights, and with tuneful and sonorous praises. The man of God, filled with tender love, stood before the manger, bathed in tears, and overflowing with joy. Solemn Masses were celebrated over the manger, Francis, the Levite of Christ, chanting the Holy Gospel. Then he preached unto the folk standing round the Birth of the King in poverty, calling Him, when he wished to name Him, the Child of Bethlehem, by reason of his tender love for Him. A certain knight, valorous and true, Messer John of Greccio, who for the love of Christ had left the secular army, and was bound by closest friendship unto the man of God, declared that he beheld a little Child right fair to see sleeping in that manger, who seemed to be awakened from sleep when the blessed Father Francis embraced Him in both arms.

The warm humanity of this reconstruction of the Nativity, in the form of an almost magical toy-like model, must have been a power in attracting the unsophisticated from pagan customs towards the Roman Church. The appeal of the doll (one recalls the Saturnalia) is universal.

The most celebrated representation of the Christ Child in this form is the *Bambino* of the church of St Maria in Aracoeli on the Capitol hill in Rome, an ancient relic of miraculous origin to whom gifts and missives are sent in thousands from all over the world. Naples also, in the eighteenth century, was a great centre of the cult of the crib. The Bourbon Charles III and his queen set the whole Court to work on the making of cribs, and one was assembled in almost every room of the palace.

In Germany the crib became a cradle that could be rocked by the devout, the *Kindelwiegen*. The worshippers thus took an exciting physical part in their devotions.

The custom has in recent years spread to churches of practically every denomination, and to some commercial establishments as well The present vigour of the tradition in Italy was recently described by a correspondent of *The Times*:

> This is the time when most Italian families are unpacking the Christmas crib to see which figures need repair or replacement. . . . Modern mass production means the loss of some of the old skills in making the figures, but this does not seem an excessive price to pay by comparison with what is happening to Christmas elsewhere: West Germans, for instance, are reported in the press here to be hanging industrial shares on their Christmas trees this year.
>
> The crib has shown an adaptability over the centuries which has allowed it to keep pace with changes of fashion and to include technological developments. . . . Purists among the supporters of the crib are at pains to keep public taste within bounds. The national association formed several years ago for this purpose draws the line, for example, at camels too large for the figures and at palm trees sprinkled with imitation snow, and insists that Christmas trees should be kept well away from the manger.
>
> This purism nevertheless encourages ingenious elaborations of the crib scene. The association's journal provides hints on how to make such diverting additions as real, miniature waterfalls. Indeed, the sort of parents who look forward to the time when they can

buy their children a model railway set can find much the same sort of enjoyment in a crib.

With a certain amount of ingenuity, illuminated stars are made to rise and fall, angels to fly, and fountains to spurt real water, which runs under bridges and turns mill wheels. . . .

Once the enthusiast has gone beyond the Holy Family, the three kings, the ox and the donkey, the field is open. Elephants have put in an appearance, though they have not yet become generally accepted. Common farmyard animals are part of the scene, as are shepherds with bagpipes, blacksmiths, innkeepers, log sawyers, water carriers and wayside sellers of bread and Neapolitan *pizze*, all set in a Bethlehem closely resembling an Italian hill village, improved perhaps with a few classical ruins.

This poetic licence and determination to transplant the Christmas story to a recognizably Italian background are philosophically approved by the purists. (Some years ago the association found nothing against a design conceived by African students incorporating jet aircraft, tanks, and atomic bombs.)

Much of the Christmas ritual, ceremony, and customs so richly used and developed by the Roman Church was dealt a blow with the coming of the Reformation in 1517. The Reformation, however, does not seem to have seriously affected British customs, which continued with vigour in Tudor times. But the Puritans disapproved, and in the time of Cromwell the celebration of the Nativity, even in the churches, was prohibited—if, as recounted by John Evelyn, sometimes ineffectually.

The general air of spiritual gloom, as distinct from physical hardship, that had enshrouded the early American settlers at Christmas can be gathered from William Bradford's *Journal* for the year 1620:

> On ye day called Christmas-day, ye Gov'r caled them out to work (as was used), but ye most of this new company excused themselves, and said it went against their consciences to work on ye day. So ye Gov'r tould them that if they made it a mater of conscience, he would spare them until they were better informed. So he led away ye rest, and left them: but when they came home at noone from their worke, he found them in ye streete at play, openly; some pitching ye barr, and some at stoole ball, and such like sports. So he went to them and tooke away their implements,

TWELFTH NIGHT.

CHRISTMAS GAMBOLS, OR A KISS UNDER THE MISTLETOE.

Top: Twelfth Night. Engraving published by Laurie & Whittle, 1794. *British Museum.*

Bottom: Christmas Gambols, or A Kiss Under the Mistletoe. Engraving published by Laurie & Whittle, 1794. *British Museum.*

Landing of the Pilgrims at Plymouth, 11 December 1620. Lithograph by Nathaniel Currier, c. 1850.

and told them it was against his conscience that they should play and others worke. If they made ye keeping of it matter of devotion, let them kepe their houses, but there should be no gameing or revelling in ye streets. Since which time nothing hath been attempted that way, at least, openly.

That was in Plymouth Colony. In 1659 Puritans of the American colonies enacted a law in the General Court of Massachusetts declaring that 'anybody who is found observing, by abstinence from labor, feasting, or any other way, any such daye as Christmas day, shall pay for every such offense five shillings'.

With the increasing entry into the country of the Church of England, and a more tolerant outlook, this law was repealed in 1681. But a strong Puritanical influence remained. Apart from matters of doctrine, the Puritans in America—like the Puritans in Britain—objected to the secular celebration of Christmas because it interfered with their religious devotions. The Puritans also associated Christmas celebrations with the English Court and the political influences which had caused them to emigrate.

After the Restoration the celebration of the Twelve Days in England never quite recovered its former elaboration. In the succeeding years a certain air of artificiality and patronage may be detected in the general attitude towards Christmas. One may cite here as evidence Addison's overquoted but still very enjoyable account of Sir Roger de Coverley's Christmas.

During the Georgian age singularly little of consequence was written about the season. Is it not significant that Samuel Johnson—so far as we can trace—never commented upon it to Boswell? But among the less genteel there is no doubt that Christmas customs were vigorously maintained. This was shown in 1752, when very belatedly Britain changed to the Gregorian Calendar, and Christmas Day, which had formerly been celebrated on what is now 6 January, was put back. *The Gentleman's Magazine* in 1753 published the following reports:

Quainton in Buckinghamshire, Dec. 24. Above 2000 came here this night, with lanthorns and candles, to view a blackthorn which grows in this neighbourhood, and which was remembered (this year only) to be a slip from the famous Glastonbury thorn, that it always budded on the 24th, and was full blown the next day, and went all off at night: but the people finding no appearance of a bud, 'twas agreed by all, that *December* 25 N.S. could not be the right *Christmas-Day*, and as accordingly refused going to church, and treating their friends on that day as usual: at length the affair became so serious, that the ministers of the neighbouring villages, in order to appease the people, thought it prudent to give notice, that the old *Christmas-Day* should be kept holy as before.

Glastonbury. A vast concourse of people attended the noted thorns on *Christmas-Eve*, New-Stile; but to their great disappointment, there was no appearance of its blowing, which made them watch it till the 5th of *Jan.*, the *Christmas-Day* Old Stile, when it blowed as usual.

At the end of the eighteenth and early in the nineteenth century the antiquarians were becoming interested in old Christmas. William Hone, for example, during the eighteen-thirties wrote with enthusiasm of the customs still surviving in Wales, which were later described more fully by Marie Trevelyan:

In the days of old, Christmastide festivities extended into several weeks. Preparations for burning the Christmas log and for the various feasts were extensive and elaborate. Then the bards and the musicians of the Principality were active, and many kinds of amusements and entertainments were arranged. Nearly all the old Christmas customs have become obsolete, but the singing and literary festivals still remain in the form of local *eisteddfodau*. The old time revelry has vanished, and with it the bringing in of the Christmas log; the quaint morris or merry dancers, with the Aderyn Pig Llwyd or 'Bird with the Grey Beak'; the Mari Llwyd, or Holy Mary; and the wassailing, amusements and festivals in connection with the New Year and Twelfth Night, or old Christmas Day. In Wales burning torches were greatly in evidence with the Christmas log.

The interest of the antiquarians spread to the expanding middle classes. That their ideas of celebration were more refined than those of their forebears is indicated by William Harrison's *The Humorist* of 1832:

Thrice welcome, Christmas! maugre thine approach
    Be mark'd by skies somewhat too cold and murky;
I hail thy harbinger, the Norwich coach,
    Laden, inside and out, with chine and turkey,
And sausage by the fathom. . . .

Where is *Snap-Dragon?* all extinguish'd—vanish'd!
Where mystic *Mistletoe?* unfairly banish'd,
    To grace the kitchen, and I live to tell it!
Where's *Blind Man's Buff?* alas! this march of mind,
With all its boasted blessings, hath refined,
    Us out of half our former recreations!

Where is old *Hunt the Slipper?* with the snow
Which melted many, many years ago.
    Where *Forfeits*, paid (I hate alliterations)
In cunning Cupid's current coinage, kisses?
Despatch'd to Coventry to modern misses.

Where are the *Country Dances*, once promoted
To such distinction in our revels? Voted
    Old fashion'd as the Laird of Batmawhapple.
'Cast off', 'Pousette,' the modish belle derides,
As figures rude as Runic ones; 'Change Sides'
    Is practised only in St Stephen's Chapel.

The new enthusiasm was fanned by the writing of Charles Dickens, his first Christmas piece being among the *Sketches by Boz*, a collection of periodical articles published in 1836. Christmas again appeared in *Pickwick Papers*. Then in 1843 was published the story with the famous opening words:

> Marley was dead, to begin with. There is no doubt about that. The register of his burial was signed by the clergyman, the clerk, the undertaker, and the chief mourner. Scrooge signed it . . .

Scrooge's name soon became good not only 'upon 'Change for anything he chose to put his hand to' but throughout the English-speaking world as an evocation of the new Christmas spirit, with its sudden transformation to universal beneficence.

Even earlier the American Washington Irving, who came to England in 1815, had written in an Addisonian vein of the English Christmas in *Geoffrey Crayon's Sketch Book* of 1820. Thackeray, a year younger than Dickens, and more subtle, became the master of the finer shades of the modes and manners of the Victorian Christmas.

Meanwhile the illustrators—George Cruikshank, John Leech, Kenny Meadows, a little later Randolph Caldecott, and countless masters of

George Cruikshank

the engraved wood block who practised their art in the pages of *Punch*, *The Illustrated London News*, and other now forgotten periodicals—brought into visual being a new Christmas world.

But it was the Queen herself who lit the lights of the new Christmas. When she married Prince Albert of Saxe-Coburg he brought with him a wealth of German Christmas lore, which the royal family practised with enthusiasm. If they were not quite the first Christmas trees in England those at Windsor Castle set an example which rapidly spread throughout the British Isles.

The panegyrists and practitioners of Christmas customs in Britain in the early nineteenth century soon spread the cult farther afield.

Christmas became widely celebrated in the Antipodes, where the sun is at its height at Christmas time. This change of climate was at first difficult to accept. Douglas Sladen in *A Christmas Letter from Australia* wrote:

> It is not quite a Christmas here with this unclouded sky,
> This pure transparent atmosphere, this sun mid-heaven-high;
> To see the rose upon the bush, young leaves upon the trees,
> And hear the forest's summer hush or the low hum of bees.

The early Dutch settlers in New York had observed the Christmas season, particularly St Nicholas' Day on 6 December, but the increasing preponderance of English settlers shifted the emphasis to 25 December. James H. Barnett summarized the position up to about 1750 thus: the communities in which Roman Catholics, Episcopalians and Dutch Reformed colonists were in the ascendancy celebrated Christmas, whereas where the Quakers, Baptists, Congregationalists and Presbyterians were dominant Christmas festivities were denigrated.

Yet the element among the early settlers that 'pitched ye barr' in Bradford's time persisted, and all the English traditional customs were in existence in America, often in a somewhat hole-and-corner manner, from the earliest times. Christmas customs were introduced also by the English and Hessian soldiers during the Revolutionary War. According to some historians the Hessians were celebrating Christmas too well in 1776, when, on the night of 25 December, General George Washington crossed the Delaware River and was thus able to surprise and defeat the garrison stationed at Trenton, New Jersey.

During the early nineteenth century both the religious and the secular celebration spread in America. Carols and Christmas hymns were more generally sung, though the giving of Christmas presents, other than charity towards the less fortunate, was unusual until much later in the century. In the eighteen-fifties there still remained religious opposition from the Puritanical organizations, whose churches were closed on 25 December. However, the Roman Catholic and other celebrating sects had for some time opened their churches, which were decked with evergreens—a custom brought from England. Even in the eighteen-thirties advertisements which appeared in journals in some of the larger American cities mentioned Christmas.

The publication of Washington Irving's English Christmas studies, Dickens's *Sketches by Boz*, *Pickwick Papers*, and particularly *A Christmas Carol* in 1843, was as influential in popularizing the 'old-fashioned' Christmas with the people of North America as in Britain. And about this time the Americans took the Dutch Santa Claus to their hearts and built him up to a great folk-figure.

The legal recognition of Christmas Day as a holiday in America was initiated by the state of Alabama in 1836; the last state to accept it was Oklahoma in 1890—though the majority of states had done so ten years before.

The influence of Dickens and the newly-furbished folk-figure of Santa Claus upon the American people in the nineteenth century is illustrated by the story of the child who, when told of Dickens's death, asked: 'Will Father Christmas die too?'

2

Evergreen Thoughts

When rosemary and bays, the Poet's crown,
Are bawl'd, in frequent cries, through all the town,
Then judge the festival of *Christmas* near,
Christmas, the joyous period of the year.
Now with bright holly all your temples strow,
With lawrel green, and sacred mistletoe.

JOHN GAY, *Trivia*, 1716

Christmas decorations—the rosemary and bays, the holly, the laurel, and the mistletoe—have a spiritual symbolism that goes far back into the past. In the northern hemisphere, towards the winter solstice:

... flowers depart,
To see their Mother-root, when they have blown;
   Where they together,
   All the hard weather,
Dead to the world, keep house unknown.

Can it be wondered that the imaginative among human beings early saw something significant in the few plants that remained green—or even bore berries—at the darkest season of the winter?

The use of evergreens and flowers for decking temples, and of garlands for decoration of the person—possibly some form of contact with the spirit of vegetation—is of the greatest antiquity. The learned have discussed it since the days of Sir Thomas Browne, and no doubt earlier. Obviously the Christian Church took over and converted to its own use many of the floral traditions which had flourished in pagan times.

One plant, however, the Church has never adopted: the mistletoe. This peculiar and pallid-berried shrub, parasitic on many trees, particularly apples, but very rarely on oaks or evergreens, was responsible for the death of Balder, the Norse god of light—the Scandinavian equivalent of Apollo. The northern gods, realizing that if harm befell the god of light it could mean their general downfall, laid everything, quick and dead, under an obligation to refrain from harming Balder. But Loki, the god of evil, learning that this vow had not been enjoined upon the mistletoe, which was considered too weak to hurt anyone, persuaded the blind god Hoder to throw a dart of mistletoe at Balder which miraculously stabbed him to death. This myth is clearly rooted in primitive tree-worship, but it may also be taken as a sun-myth, denoting the overcoming of the powers of light by the forces of winter.

Writing in the first century, Pliny gives us the well-known account of a white-robed Druid climbing an oak-tree, armed with a golden sickle, and cutting a branch which fell into a white cloth. The sprigs were distributed as a charm against evil.

Mistletoe was a devilfuge, an all-heal. It was given to the cow that calved just after New Year's Day, to avert ill-luck from the herd. It had many other symbolic uses. But from the earliest times it was never allowed inside a church (though it is represented in the carving on a tomb of the Berkeleys in Bristol Cathedral). The reason for this may be partly a mistrust of its pagan associations, or it may be connected with the belief, held by the Bretons, that mistletoe was originally a tree and was the timber used for the Cross—since when, in shame, it has shrunk to a feeble parasitic shrub.

The custom of kissing under the mistletoe is English in origin, perhaps a vestige of the licence of ancient folk-festivals. The making of 'kissing bunches', elaborate hanging structures of evergreens, rosy-cheeked apples, paper flowers, and dolls representing Joseph, Mary, and the infant Jesus, probably had the same origin. In recent years the making and display of kissing bunches or kissing 'boughs' has been revived in Britain and in North America as a native English custom long pre-dating the cult of the exotic Christmas spruce tree.

Here is Laurence Whistler's description of the construction of the Kissing Bough so exquisitely depicted by him in the glass engraving illustrated overleaf:

Andrew Dunn. Christmas. c. 1830. Messrs. Thomas Agnew & Sons, Ltd

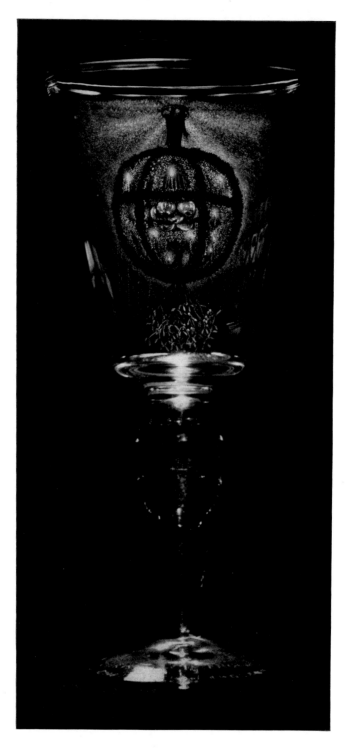

Laurence Whistler (b. 1907). Kissing Bough. Diamond-point engraving on glass, 1960.

Five equal circles of thickish, not too pliable wire, say 1 ft. 9 ins. in diameter, are bound together so that one becomes the horizontal 'equator', with the four others crossing at the 'poles', to form eight 'meridians', equally spaced. The frame is then wound with insulating tape, to give a rougher surface for binding on the evergreen, preferably box, which will thickly cover it all over. In the exact centre, seven red apples hang on red ribbons (taken right through the core with a bodkin and knotted below, if the stalks are gone). Eight red candles are clipped in the spaces round the 'equator'. Another eight rise from the 'meridians' half-way towards the bottom. (Permanent candle-holders for these are fastened to the frame. They are shaped by twisting the free end of each short piece of wire round the end of a pencil.) Finally the device is hung up, on red cords perhaps, and the mistletoe is tied beneath.

Although mistletoe abounds in the western, south-western, and a few other parts of Britain, many tons are imported annually from France, mostly cut in Brittany. In Australia (except Tasmania) the local form of mistletoe is so abundant as to be a dangerous forest weed; it is not there used for decoration.

If the spiritual qualities of mistletoe are rather dubious, holly (or holme), whose symbolic antecedents were equally pagan, has become entirely respectable. In Restoration times John Evelyn, who loved this 'incomparable' tree above all evergreens, was puzzled why the ancient writer Macrobius included it among 'unfortunate' plants. But he goes on to recall that other writers put it

> among the *Lucky*, for so it seems they used to send Branches of it, as well as of *Oak* (the most *fortunate*, according to the *Gentile Theology*) with their *Strenae* (New Year's Gifts) begun (as *Symachus* tells us) by K. *Tatius*, almost as old as Rome herself.
>
> But to say no more of these *superstitious Fopperies*, which are many other about this Tree, we still dress up both our *Churches and Houses*, on *Christmas* and other Festival Days, with its cheerful *green* and *rutilant Berries*.

Since the days of 'superstitious fopperies' holly has attracted to itself much Christian lore, and, as the red berries connect it with the Passion, it is known in Scandinavian countries as 'Christ-thorn'.

Once holly was held to be in opposition to the ivy. A reason given for this was that the holly belonged to the Christian home and church, the Bacchanalian ivy to the inn. Another explanation was that the holly was male and sturdy, the ivy female and clinging.

Another type of tree sometimes but not always connected with Christmas has its legendary origin in the staff of a saint which, stuck into the ground by its bearer in a moment of despair, burgeoned and flowered. The most famous of such miraculous trees is the Glastonbury thorn.

The legend is that when Joseph of Arimathaea came to Britain, bringing with him the Christian faith, he landed on the Isle of Avalon, famed in the Arthurian legend. The old man, fatigued with the climb up a steep hill, and, no doubt, depressed by the trying prospect of con-verting the natives, plunged his staff into the ground. The day was Christmas Eve. Suddenly the staff, which was of hawthorn, broke into leaf and flower. It was a sign of encouragement to Joseph, and to all those who beheld it, of the miraculous power of his faith. When Glaston-bury Abbey was built nearby, the thorn, now rooted, was transferred within its precincts.

Dean Armitage Robinson, the great authority on Glastonbury, has unearthed the first record of the thorn, which 'do burge and bere greene leaves at Christmas' and 'groweth in Werall'. This was written about 1502. The hill which Joseph is reputed to have climbed is still known as Wearyall Hill.

In 1613 Michael Drayton wrote of the 'three times famouse Ile' of Glastonbury, famed for 'great Arthur's tomb', 'holy Joseph's grave', and where 'trees yet in winter bloome, and bear their Summer's green'. Not until 1635, with the visit of Sir William Brereton, do we get a full and first-hand account of the tree, 'so famous and so much visited and frequented on the day of Christ's nativity'. It then grew half a mile from Glastonbury.

Sir William collected branches and leaves, and carved his initials on the trunk, at the same time observing that the tree was in a bad way because his many predecessors had done likewise! He censured the local inhabitants for not taking proper care of it. A number of grafts had at divers times been taken, one forming a notable tree at a tavern near the George ('whereof also I brought away with me some branches').

In the same year, Lieutenant Hammond of Norwich inspected the thorn, and also the one at the tavern, which, after a 'glass of good sacke', he reported as 'springing and flourishing' when he passed on his way.

About the same time we hear something of the dire effects of cutting this holy tree. James Howell, in his curious tract, *Dodona's Grove, or the Vocall Forest*, considered that: 'He was well served of his blind zeal, who, going to cut down an ancient white hawthorn-tree, which because she budded before others, might be an occasion of superstition, had some of the prickles flew into his eye, and made him monocular.'

John Parkinson in 1640 refers to '*Spina acuta biflora Britanica*, England's Hawthorn'. He tells us that this 'grows in divers places in our land, where it is not greatly wondered at by those who live there'. He names trees at Glastonbury Abbey, at High Street or Whey Street in Romney Marsh, and near Nantwich in Cheshire.

In 1646 Sir Thomas Browne pointed out that precociousness is known in many trees other than the 'Glassenbury' thorn, and 'strange effects are naturally taken for miracles by weaker heads'. He adds: 'Such a thorn there is in Parham Park, Suffolk, and elsewhere.'

That industrious Victorian authoress, Agnes Strickland, unearthed in France an account of a Christmas spent at the Court of Charles II by Père Cyprian Gamache in 1660. Christmas, he tells us, is always celebrated in England with greater pomp than in any other European realm. Flowers of the Glastonbury thorn, which usually flowers on Christmas Eve, are brought up in procession on Christmas morning and presented to the King and Queen. This thorn, says Father Gamache, was much venerated by the English, who told him that St Joseph of Arimathaea brought to Glastonbury a thorn out of our Lord's Crown, and placed it in the earth. Thenceforth it blossomed on Christmas Day.

In more recent times the most interesting development is the spreading of this cult, while still maintained at Glastonbury, to Herefordshire. In the mid-nineteenth century there appear to have been no less than eleven hawthorn trees in that county which were venerated. Today, at Christmas, one or more of the several that still remain is regularly visited by a reporter and a press photographer. There are, of course, offspring from the original Glastonbury tree growing in botanical and private gardens, but some at least of the Herefordshire trees are in quite remote places and it seems improbable that all of them derive from Glastonbury.

Botanically, the tree is *Crataegus monogyna biflora*. Parkinson, you will note, used the name *biflora*. It is a form of the common hawthorn that produces two batches of flower buds. The first can be seen developing in autumn. They are usually ready to open about Christmas time, particularly if a few mild days occur, as they often do at that season. It is perhaps relevant to mention that the tree seems to flower more reluctantly now in the cold light of electric torches than it did when scrutinized under the warm glow of a hundred lanterns.

In spring, *biflora* produces another crop of normal flowers. This phenomenon is also found in other trees. There is, for instance, a flowering cherry, Jugatsu Sakura (*Prunus subhirtella autumnalis*), from Japan, quite often seen in our gardens. This usually blooms rather earlier than the Glastonbury thorn, and far outdoes our native phenomenon in beauty. One day it too may enter the Christmas *flora*.

The fame of the Glastonbury thorn and other miraculous flowering trees is not comparable with that originating from the European spruce fir, which in little more than a century has carried the custom of erecting a Christmas tree to most parts of the world. Before considering the Christmas tree, however, let us spare a word for rosemary, which was given pride of place by all writers on Christmas decorations from the fourteenth to the middle of the nineteenth century, but is now sadly neglected. To the generally beneficent qualities of rosemary herbalists testify from ancient days onwards. Particularly it is Shakespeare's 'Rosemary, that's for remembrance' and a herb that keeps 'seeing and savour all the winter long'.

'As for Rosmarine,' wrote that ardent gardener Sir Thomas More, 'I lett it runne all over my garden walls, not onlie because my bees love it, but because 'tis the herb sacred to remembrance, and therefore to friendship. . . .' Today, however (perhaps because it is not everywhere a hardy plant), rosemary is seldom to be seen among Christmas decorations. And the boar's head, which it used to beautify, is even more out of fashion.

One herb that was once famous is now even more forgotten than rosemary. In the seventeenth century it was described very frankly by Sir Thomas Browne:

> The Rose of Jericho, that flourishes every year just about Christmas Eve, is famous in Christian reports; which, notwithstanding we have some reason to doubt, and are plainly informed by Bellonius, it is but a Monastical imposture, as he hath delivered in his observations, concerning the plants in Jericho. That which promoted the conceit or perhaps begot its continuance, was a propriety in this plant. For though it be dry, yet will it upon imbibition of moisture dilate its leaves, and explicate its flowers contracted, and seemingly dried up. And this is to be effected not only in the Plant yet growing, but in some manner also in that which is brought exuccuous and dry unto us. Which quality being observed, the subtilty of contrivers did commonly play this shew upon the Eve of our Saviour's Nativity, when by drying the Plant again, it closed the next day, and so pretended a double mystery: referring unto the opening and closing of the womb of Mary.

The botanists are even more succinct, describing this miraculous rose as a small annual cruciferous plant, native of western Asia and north-eastern Africa, whose dried fronds unfurl under the influence of moisture.

The original Christmas tree, it is charmingly said, was devised by Martin Luther in the early years of the sixteenth century. One Christmas Eve he was walking under a brilliant star-lit sky. The snowy, frosted fir trees sparkled in the moonlight; his thoughts turned to the Nativity. Coming back to his home he tried with a sapling to reconstruct the scene, representing the star-light with candles.

Considering the Christmas tree more factually, the use of the fir (*Tannenbaum*) seems to have originated at the winter solstice celebrations of the pagan German tribes in the Black Forest; it was well and widely established by Martin Luther's time. Probably not until the end of the seventeenth century did it carry lights. The custom was

Queen Victoria's Christmas tree, 1848.
Engraving from the *Illustrated London News*.

essentially a German one, spreading through the fir-clad Scandinavian countries and reaching America when Hessian soldiers were engaged in the Revolution. (Indeed, there is evidence of a Christmas tree being in use by German settlers in Pennsylvania as early as 1746.)

It may come as a surprise to English readers to know that the cult of the Christmas tree was familiar in the United States before it was known in much of Europe. It spread to France from Germany in the early nineteenth century. German merchants and Court officials brought it to England in the late 1820s. Princess Lieven had trees at Panshanger in 1829. The custom was, in fact, known and described in England before the occasion that made it, almost overnight, a major part of the British Christmas celebrations—the marriage of pretty little Queen Victoria to Prince Albert of Saxe-Coburg in 1840. The Prince, of course, brought the tree and its traditions with him. How soon it became established in the royal home can be judged from this account in *The Illustrated London News* of 1848:

> The Christmas tree in the engraving [*on facing page*] is that which is annually prepared by her Majesty's command for the Royal children. . . . The tree employed for this festive purpose is a young fir of about eight feet high, and has six tiers of branches. On each tier, or branch, are arranged a dozen wax tapers. Pendant from the branches are elegant trays, baskets, *bonbonnières*, and other receptacles for sweetmeats of the most varied and expensive kind; and of all forms, colours and degrees of beauty. Fancy cakes, gilt gingerbread and eggs filled with sweetmeats, are also suspended by variously-coloured ribbons from the branches. The tree, which stands upon a table covered with white damask, is supported at the root by piles of sweets of a larger kind, and by toys and dolls of all descriptions, suited to the youthful fancy, and to the several ages of the interesting scions of Royalty for whose gratification they are displayed.
>
> The trees are constructed and arranged by Mr Mawdill, the Queen's confectioner.

The Christmas tree, erected and embellished in the manner of the British royal household, spread rapidly over the fast developing British

Empire, and was introduced to scenes and climes incongruously different from the dark Rhenish forests whence it came.

The spruce fir is not a native of the British Isles, but has long been cultivated for its timber. The demand for Christmas trees became so great that young trees were imported from the Continent in large numbers. With the emergence of British commercial forestry early in the present century the cultivation of spruce trees especially for the purpose—quite a difficult undertaking—became a profitable side-line. Their production now is on a vast scale.

Though in Europe the spruce fir is universally used, this tree is not grown in the land where the cult of the Christmas tree is now at its most extravagant—the United States. The rich and varied sylva of the North American continent is, however, reflected in a like variety of Christmas trees. Several kinds of conifer are used, and one, the Douglas fir, provided the biggest* Christmas tree on record. Set up by the Northgate community, a shopping centre near Seattle, Washington, it stood 212 feet high and weighed 25 tons.

At Hilton Park, Wilmington, N.C., an ancient, though very living, oak provides a permanent Christmas tree. At the due season it displays 7,000 coloured lights, and from its boughs are draped six tons of Spanish moss. The White House has a National Living Christmas Tree, its illuminations lit each year by the President.

In other lands, too, trees of varying kinds are known as Christmas trees. New Zealand has one that goes under that name because of the red flowers which open in December and January; its native name is Pohutakawa. In exposed places it assumes a fantastic shape, like a Japanese *bonsai*.

The decoration of the Christmas tree has changed radically from its early form in one respect only—electric lights of all colours have superseded the guttering (and sometimes rather alarming) candle flames. Toys, of course, are still toys, though their nature changes from year to year. A delightful custom increasingly in favour is to display the illumined tree in a window facing the street.

The Christmas rose is a true Christmas flower, though it is also

* It may now have been exceeded.

Illuminated Christmas Tree at the White House, Washington.

Christmas Rose (*Helleborus niger*). Coloured engraving in Curtis's *Botanical Magazine*, 1793.

associated, because of its pure flower and the date of its opening, with St Agnes, the patroness of purity, whose day is 21 January. Reginald Farrer wrote of its other name, black hellebore, that it was 'so called because its heart, or root, is black, while its face shines with a blazing white innocence, unknown to the truly pure of heart'. It is a plant that comes from the mountainous districts of central Europe. In Germany it is called *Christwurz*.

There are, of course, many kinds of hellebore—but we are inclined to agree with Parkinson who wrote in the early seventeenth century that this was the 'true and right kinde, whose flowers have the most beautifull aspect, and at the time of flowering most rare, that is, in the deepe of Winter about Christmas, when no other can be seen upon the ground....'

Until the beginning of the present century it was cultivated on a considerable scale for the Christmas trade. There were several Christmas rose farms, particularly in Cheshire, from which thousands were sold. There is no growing thing which we would more gladly see restored to a place of pride in the bouquet of Christmas than this plant, so delicately described by Gerald Bullett:

> Wing'd blossom of white thought, yellow-centred
> Star of fertility sprung from December soil,
> Six perfect petal-rays of frozen light:
>
> See, under the stark oak, in her nest
> Of long, serrated, green, environing leaves,
> Where like a bird she listens and looks out,
>
> See now, at twilight, how her pale presence,
> Even between sundown and dawning star,
> Fills the dusk with quickness, quiet as prayer.

It has always been the general custom that decorations be removed after Epiphany. Some people, however, have held that they should remain until the Eve of the Purification of the Blessed Virgin Mary, or Candlemas, which falls on 2 February. Such a belief was long held in Shropshire, where the holly and ivy, on being taken down, were re-placed by snowdrops, the 'Candlemas bells'.

The different forms that Christmas church decorations have taken are no doubt haphazard even if traditional. This was not good enough for the systematic Victorians, and in 1859 the Rev. Edward L. Cutts, B.A., put this sad state of affairs right by the publication of a vigorous yet tactful *Essay on the Christmas Decoration of Churches*. It was obviously written to counteract a not insignificant feeling against the relics of paganism; he was careful to point out and emphasize the frequent use of foliage in Gothic church sculpture.

After detailing the virtues and decorative possibilities of holly, ivy, laurel, yew, arbor-vitae, myrtle, and box, Mr Cutts continues:

> Shall we use Flowers in our decorations? There are a great number of excellent persons, who like to see the Church decorated with the customary Christmas greenery, but have a horror of the introduction of flowers; it is a novelty, and they suspect all novelties. . . .
>
> The fact remains that, reason or no reason, there are a considerable number of excellent and worthy persons who will admit that there is no abstract objection to the introduction of a few flowers among the decorations; they even think there would be something poetical and beautiful in putting a great bouquet upon the Communion Table—if there were no superstitious intention in it; but, in these days of change, they are afraid of every novelty; they fear lest too much regard be had to these things, in themselves innocent; they fear the gradual and insidious return of superstitious practices; they fear a serpent lying hid among your flowers. Take care, dear Decorators, that you do not give good reason for such fears.

From early times—for example in the Italian *presèpio*—artificial as opposed to living materials were used in decoration. With the increased popularity of the Christmas tree their production became professional. A large trade developed in angels, fairies, flags, fragile glass ornaments of dazzling colours and curious shapes, glittering stars and soft streamers of tinsel, netted bags of sweetmeats, and strings of American popcorn blown-up from maize.

One of the latest accessories to be invented was the now universal Christmas cracker. It seems that it originated in a French device, a bag of bon-bons enclosed in a paper covering that must be tugged hard by two children before it burst open to release the contents. (The French were at first the master-makers of these novelties.) We have failed to find any evidence of the existence of the modern explosive cracker before 1860, but it seems that about that time an English firm adopted the French device and added a minute explosion at the moment the two parts split asunder. Fancy paper hats, mottoes, and a myriad of small toys have subsequently been enclosed within increasingly elaborate, decorated (and expensive) crackers.

By 1900 cracker making had become a minor industry, as we can read in *The New Penny Magazine* of that year:

> Fifteen floors, most of them a hundred feet long and twenty-five feet wide, and all of them given up to sweet-stuff and Christmas crackers! ...
>
> See those piles of parcels stacked from floor to ceiling, and completely filling some of the vast floors, except for narrow gangways for passing through them. There are hundreds of thousands of these boxes, and every box is stuffed full of glittering crackers, every cracker itself containing some curious object in the heart of it— an article of jewellery, a little illustrated book, a flexible face, a night-cap, a royal crown, a bottle of hair dye, a trumpet, a pack of cards, a harp, a fountain of scent, a bunch of magic flowers, a monkey, a piece of wedding cake, a mask, or a mirror. . . .
>
> The old fashion style of cracker was very simple. But crackers in these aesthetic times of ours are works of art, and the best of them, at least, now present pictorial embellishments which would not disgrace South Kensington.

3

Gifts and Remembrances

It is taken for granted in English-speaking and German-speaking countries that Christmas Day is the supreme day of the year for the giving of gifts. In France and some other countries the day for presentation is more often New Year's Day. In neither case is the choice of day very logical from a Christian point of view, since the gift-giving which we are assumed to be commemorating is that of the Magi, and that occurred on the Twelfth Day—now 6 January—a day not now concerned with the giving of presents except for the Santa Claus-like but female figure of the Befana in Italy, who brings gifts to good children during the preceding night.

There seem to be at least two strands of pagan tradition woven into our present-giving. From the north come several winter festivals, perpetuated in such Christian feasts as those of St Martin and St Nicholas, which fall before the Twelve Days but which to a considerable extent (possibly for economic reasons) have now been drawn within their orbit. The other strand comes from the south, from the Saturnalia and even more directly from the January Kalends—with their *strenae* now modernized as *étrennes*. These owe their name originally to boughs plucked from the grove of the goddess Strenia, who presided over the gifts at that season: it is said that the custom originated in a wish to propitiate the spirit of vegetation.

Various motives, traditional and personal, underlie the giving of gifts. There are the gifts brought to good children by mythical personages. There are presents given out of charity to the poor or unfortunate, which are quite distinct from the presents given by relative to relative or friend to friend. In the United States, for example, the former were given some years before the latter, which were scarcely known in the early nineteenth century. Finally, there is the monetary gift expected by employees or those rendering some regular service—a gift traditionally made on Boxing Day.

The problems of present-giving were discussed with sophistication by the poet Martial in the first century:

> You have sent me at the Saturnalia, Umber, all the presents you have collected in five days; twelve three-leaved tablets and seven tooth-picks, accompanied by a sponge, half a peck of beans, a wicker crate of Picenian olives, and a black flagon of Laletanian must: and with these some small Syrian figs, dried prunes, and a jar heavy with the weight of Libyan figs. I scarcely think the whole lot worth thirty sesterces, yet eight hulking Syrians carried it. How much more conveniently, and with no labour, might a boy have brought five pounds of silver plate!

Equally urbane and disillusioned was Saki's 'knut', Reginald, a typical young man-about-town of the early years of the twentieth century:

> There ought to be technical education classes on the science of present-giving. No one seems to have the faintest notion of what any one else wants, and prevalent ideas on the subject are not creditable to a civilized community.
>
> There is, for instance, the female relative in the country who 'knows a tie is always useful', and sends you some spotted horror that you could only wear in secret or in the Tottenham Court Road. It *might* have been useful if she had kept it to tie up currant bushes with, when it would have served the double purpose of supporting the branches and frightening away the birds. . . .
>
> Then there are aunts. They are always a difficult class to deal with in the matter of presents. The trouble is that one never catches them really young enough. By the time one has educated them to an appreciation of the fact that one does not wear red woollen mittens in the West End, they die, or quarrel with the family, or do something equally inconsiderate. . . .

There is one almost universal Christmas custom of a secular kind—perhaps the only one—that has no trace of pre-Christian origin. It is dependent on the relatively modern craft of printing and the efficient systems of postal communication that have grown up within little more than a century. The sending of remembrances by means of a decorated card is, indeed, closely bound up with the reforms of the British Post Office brought about by Sir Rowland Hill. These began in the year 1836, when the rates of postage for a single-sheet letter ranged from 4*d.* to 1*s.* 8*d.*: and culminated on 10 January 1840, when a uniform penny rate came into being throughout the United Kingdom.

The originator of the first Christmas card as we now know it has been the subject of some discussion, but it seems almost beyond doubt that it was Henry (later Sir Henry) Cole (1808–82), a civil servant who was much concerned with the Post Office reforms and also with the Great Exhibition of 1851 and the foundation of the Victoria and Albert Museum. He suggested the idea to the artist John Calcott Horsley, who made a design. This was printed by lithography, hand-coloured, and sold at a shilling a copy for Christmas 1843. Possibly a thousand were issued. The second Christmas card produced seems to have been one designed by William Maw Egley in 1848, and etched on copper.

Both cards show Christmas scenes framed in a rustic-work design through which clamber the vine leaves of conviviality. Egley's design was the first to include those two stock-in-trades of a myriad of subsequent cards, holly and mistletoe. Both cards express wishes for merriness at Christmas and happiness in the New Year. Neither, beyond displaying scenes of Christmas charity, gave any indication of the spiritual or religious meaning of the season.

Subsequent Christmas greetings mostly took the form of appropriately engraved letter-headings, or small cards rather like decorated visiting-cards. A considerable expansion took place in 1870 when the postcard was introduced to travel at half the postage rate—even if enclosed in an unsealed envelope. The development of chromolithography at this period also cheapened production of cards in gaudy colours. A little later tobacconists, toy-shops and drapers took up their sale, in addition to stationers and booksellers, and mass production began.

To enumerate the artists and printers employed at this stage is a task suited only to collectors and experts such as Mr George Buday, author of *The History of the Christmas Card* (1954). The seriousness with which the new fashion was taken is, however, illustrated by the enterprise of the firm of Hildesheimer and Faulkner who arranged a competition and exhibition of designs in 1882. The prizes amounted to £5,000. Critics remarked on the improvement of taste brought about by the general habit of card sending. It is surprising that the influence of the Valentine, which, printed or hand-made, preceded the Christmas card (it was generally delivered by hand) was so little to be seen (though it is evident in the example illustrated opposite page 44). The Valentine was of two kinds, the one exquisitely wrought and sentimental, the other coarse and exceedingly crude. The slightly comic Christmas card has long been known, but the really vulgar one is practically non-existent. However, the space for the written message *can* be used for nefarious words, as was the case with the self-conscious Mr Pooter, who wrote in his *Diary of a Nobody* some seventy years ago:

> *December* 24. I am a poor man, but I would gladly give ten shillings to find out who sent me the insulting Christmas card I received this morning. I never insult people, why should they insult me? The worst part of the transaction is, that I find myself suspecting all my friends. The handwriting on the envelope is evidently disguised, being written sloping the wrong way. I cannot think either Gowing or Cummings would do such a mean thing. Lupin denied all knowledge of it and I believe him; although I disapprove of his laughing and sympathising with the offender. Mr Franching would be above such an act; and I don't think any of the Mutlars would descend to such a course. I wonder if Pitt, that impudent clerk at the office, did it? Or Mrs Birrell, the charwoman, or Burwin-Fosselton? The writing is too good for the former.

In America cards were not at first much used. The first serious producer was Louis Prang, a skilful lithographer, who was highly successful with scenes of the Nativity, Santa Claus, children, pretty girls and subjects such as birds and butterflies. He began to market them in Boston in 1875, but by 1890 the importation of cheap cards from Europe, particularly Germany, had spoiled his market. From the 1870s, indeed, large quantities of cards were printed in France, Germany and elsewhere on the Continent and exported.

Of the variety of Christmas cards there has been no end. Cards that unfold and stand erect to form a tableau, say, of the Nativity; cards that form in a similar manner a small stage scene; cards that spread out to form fans of flowers—countless such delights were produced, particularly in later Victorian days. In 1915 the Medici Society launched their series, most beautifully printed, of Old Master reproductions. Artists of every type and style have designed cards, and the camera in due course was brought into use.

Holly, mistletoe, Santa Claus and pictures of 'ye old Christmas dinner' inevitably predominate. Very popular, also, are coaching scenes —the coach being usually snow-bound. These, it is said, enshrine almost as a folk memory the great snowstorm of 1836, which brought disaster to many of the coaches bearing the Christmas mails.

Possibly the most interesting and certainly one of the commonest Christmas card figures is the robin. Its boldness and friendliness would seem to be sufficient reason for the popularity of this bright-eyed and scarlet-waistcoated bird, and its use on Christmas cards. But, it seems, the matter is not quite so simple as that. In western Europe the robin is linked with ancient beliefs: at one time it had, because of its red breast, the reputation of being a 'fire-bringer', one of the birds that brought fire to earth. It is linked in folk-lore with the wren. There are many rhymes that vary from place to place but whose gist is:

> Kill a robin or a wren
> Never prosper boy or man.

The robin was involved in the wren hunt, though the robin itself was not hunted. One version of the hunting song was:

> We hunted the Wren for Robin the Bobbin,
> We hunted the Wren for Jack of the Can,
> We hunted the Wren for Robin the Bobbin,
> We hunted the Wren for Everyman.

At one time the robin and the wren were not infrequently seen together on Christmas cards, thus perpetuating the legendary connexion,

Mid-Victorian folding Christmas card. *Victoria and Albert Museum.*

Victorian self-erecting Christmas card. Photograph by W. T. Jones.

but this is a feature that has disappeared. It should be mentioned, incidentally, that the British robin and the robin of North America are not related.

There is another reason for introducing the robin on Christmas stationery—it was used as a symbol of the early postmen, who, dressed in uniforms bearing the royal red, were sometimes called 'Robin Postman'.

The production of Christmas cards has now become a minor industry. In the United States it has been estimated that in the early nineteen-fifties some 1,500,000,000 cards, worth a hundred million dollars, were despatched. In Britain in 1960 a figure of 577,000,000 was suggested. Are we today satisfied with the Christmas card? Christopher Morley, writing, so long ago as 1919, of American designs, expressed that uneasiness which many of us feel:

> This is an age of strange and stirring beauty, of extraordinary romance and adventure, of new joys and pains. And yet our Christmas artists have nothing more to offer us than the old formalism of Yuletide convention. After a considerable amount of searching in the bazaars we have found not one Christmas card that showed even a glimmering of the true romance, which is to see the beauty or wonder or peril that lies around us. Most of the cards hark back to the stage-coach up to its hubs in snow, or the blue bird, with which Maeterlinck penalized us (what has a blue bird got to do with Christmas?), or the open fireplace and jug of mulled claret. Now these things are merry enough in their way, or they were once upon a time; but we plead for an honest romanticism in Christmas cards that will express something of the entrancing color and circumstance that surround us to-day. Is not a commuter's train, stalled in a drift, far more lively to our hearts than the mythical stage-coach? Or an inter-urban trolley winging its way through the dusk like a casket of golden light? Or even a country flivver, loaded down with parcels and holly and the Yuletide keg of root beer? Root beer may be but meager flaggonage compared to mulled claret, but at any rate 'tis honest, 'tis actual, 'tis tangible and potable. And where, among all the Christmas cards, is the airplane, that most marvelous and heart-seizing of all our triumphs? Where is the stately apartment house, looming like

Gibraltar, against a sunset sky? Must we, even at Christmas time, fool ourselves with a picturesqueness that is gone, seeing nothing of what is around us? . . .

What could be more absurd than to send to a friend in a city apartment a rhyme such as this:

> *As around the Christmas fire you sit*
> *And hear the bells with frosty chime,*
> *Think, friendship that long love has knit*
> *Grows sweeter still at Christmas time!*

If that is sent to the janitor or the elevator boy we have no cavil, for these gentlemen do actually see a fire and hear bells ring; but the apartment tenant hears naught but the hissing of the steam in the radiator, and counts himself lucky to hear that. Why not be honest and say to him:

> *I hope the Janitor has shipped*
> *You steam, to keep the cold away;*
> *And if the hallboys have been tipped,*
> *Then joy be thine on Christmas Day!*

4

The Feast

In northern latitudes the present Christmas feast may well be in the tradition of some pagan celebration, held originally in November, and later transferred to the Nativity. The cottager has from time immemorial killed his pig in November, a circumstance often linked with an ancient sacrifice but quite certainly related to the simple fact that by that month the pigs have consumed the last of the mast—the acorns and beech-nuts—on which they fattened in the woods.

Even so, it has been pointed out that the very old custom of holding fat stock shows and dressing butchers' windows just before the Christmas season has something of the nature of a ritual display. This custom—now somewhat diminished—was described in *Punch* in 1850; described, indeed, only incidentally, as part of a bitter attack on the brutality of the conditions still obtaining:

> Nearly all the streets of London last week were more or less hung with prize beef. Tallow chandlers and soap boilers, as they looked upon the carcases, paid homage to the fat, and cooks and kitchen maids dropped curtsies to perquisites in perspective. But of all the show-beef exhibited, no carcase so worthily appealed to the admiration of a discriminating public as the carcase of an ox, destined, as we heard, for the Lord Mayor's table during the dinner festivities of the season—it was no other than the carcase of the bullock that, driven from Smithfield Market, broke shop windows, knocked down horses, and in Bowling-Green lane lifted an old woman 'into the air several feet, letting her fall near the walls' of an appropriate burial ground, which, as a final tenant, she narrowly escaped. Further, the bullock gored a man named Thomas Lagan, who two days afterwards died in St Bartholomews.
> It will be readily conceded that this bullock was—especially for

the City of London—the prize bullock of the season, as vindicating the civic wisdom that clings to Smithfield Market as a no less vital than venerable institution.

The pig rather than the ox was the traditional source of Christmas meat. In romantic descriptions of the feast the bringing in of the boar's head is always mentioned as if the creature was the wild boar of the forests. In Britain, however, that animal is believed to have become extinct during, or even before, the time of Henry II, who died in 1185.

There is the carol on bringing in the boar's head, 'used before Christmas Prince, at St John Baptist's College, Oxford, Christmas, 1607', as reprinted by William Sandys in 1833:

> The Boare is dead,
> Loe, heare is his head,
> > What man could haue done more
> Then his head of to strike,
> Meleager like,
> > And bringe it as I do before?
>
> He liuinge spoyled
> Where good men toyled,
> > Which makes kind Ceres sorrye;
> But now, dead and drawne,
> Is very good brawne,
> > And wee haue brought it for ye.
>
> Then sette downe ye Swineyard,*
> The foe to ye Vineyard,
> > Let Bacchus crowne his fall,
> Let this Boares-head and mustard
> Stand for Pigg, Goose and Custard,
> > And so ye are welcome all.

There are other old songs of this type. One refers to decking the head with 'garlands gay and rosemary'. At Queen's College, Oxford, a boar's head is still brought in with ceremony and singing, decorated with sprigs of rosemary and bay and bearing an orange in its mouth. Is this

* Swineyard: swineherd, i.e. the boar that was master of the herd.

Kenny Meadows. Making the Christmas pudding. Two drawings in the *Illustrated London News*, 1848.

A Turkey. Miniature painting of the period of Shah Jahan (1627–58)
Fitzwilliam Museum, Cambridge.

connected, perhaps, with some ancient sacrificial rite, and comparable in origins with the decking of carcases that has only lately fallen into disuse in butchers' shops?

In more recent times the boar's head has been displaced as the great Christmas dish by the turkey. There seems no authentic reason why this exotic bird, sombre in its dark and crimson, profound and dignified in its appearance until it emits that unfortunate 'gobble, gobble, gobble', should have achieved this particular fame. It is a native of Mexico and North America generally, where huge flocks used to roam when Europeans first observed it. It was probably imported to Spain fairly soon after the discovery of Mexico in 1518. There is an accurate picture made of it in 1555 by Pierre Belon, the French naturalist, and the extent of its travels is shown by a fine Mogul miniature painting, belonging to the period of Shah Jahan (1627–58), now in the Fitzwilliam Museum at Cambridge. Traditionally the bird was first brought to England by William Strickland, whose crest granted in about 1550 is a turkey-cock. The actual date has been placed between 1524 and 1532, but there is some doubt about early records of its service as a meal since it may have been confused with the guinea fowl. Certainly turkey was served at table as early as 1590. It was at first known as the Ind-cock and the Indian peacock. In France it was *poulet d'Inde*—hence *dindon*.

Quite early in the seventeenth century turkey was becoming a special Christmas dish. George II kept as many as 3,000 in Richmond Park—to shoot. Bewick in 1797 gives us an idea of the large scale on which turkeys were already farmed:

> Turkies are bred in great numbers in Norfolk, Suffolk and other counties, from which whence they are driven to the London markets in flocks of several hundreds each. The drivers manage them with great facility, by means of a bit of red rag tied to a long pole, which, from the antipathy these birds bear to that colour, acts as a scourge, and effectually answers the purpose.

The British have a particular reputation for heavy feeding at Christmas time. An Italian saying is, or was, used of a very busy person: 'Ha più da fare che i forni di Natale in Inghilterra'—'He has more to do than the ovens in England at Christmas.' Certainly, Henri Misson in his *Mémoires d'Angleterre* of 1699 was impressed by British Christmas puddings:

> Dans toutes les Familles, on fait a Noël un fameux Pâté, qu'on apelle le Pâté de Noël. C'est un grande Science que le composition de ce Pâté; c'est un docte hachis de Langue de Boeuf, de blanc de Volaille, d'Oeufs, de Sucre, de raisins de Corinthe, d'écorce de Citron & d'Orange, de diverses sortes d'épiceries, &c, &c. On fait aussi une certaine sorte de potage avec des raisins, qui ne céde point au Pâté; cela s'apelle Plum-Porridge.

The use of the word 'plum' joined with 'pudding' is curious. Probably it refers to the dried plums or prunes used before the introduction of raisins, which replaced them; but the old name continued to be used. The *Oxford Dictionary* gives a delightful quotation dated 1660:

> . . . He that discovered the new star in Cassiopeia . . . deserves not half so much to be remembered, as he that first married minced meat and raisins together.

The proportion of meat has, we assume, considerably decreased.

The ritual and glory of the Victorian plum pudding were emotionally described in the *Illustrated London News* of 1848:

> In a household where there are five or six children, the eldest not above ten or eleven, the making of the pudding is indeed an event. It is thought of days, if not weeks, before. To be allowed to share in the noble work, is a prize for young ambition. . . . Lo! the lid is raised, curiosity stands on tip-toe, eyes sparkle with anticipation, little hands are clapped in extasy, almost too great to find expression in words. 'The hour arrives—the moment wished and feared;' —wished, oh! how intensely; feared, not in the event, but lest envious fate should not allow it to be an event, and mar the glorious concoction in its very birth.
>
> And then when it is dished, when all fears of this kind are over, when the roast beef has been removed, when the pudding, in all the glory of its own splendour, shines upon the table, how eager is the anticipation of the near delight! How beautifully it steams! How delicious it smells! How round it is! A kiss is round, the

horizon is round, the earth is round, the moon is round, the sun and stars, and all the host of heaven are round. So is plum pudding.

Much more international are cakes, pastries (such as the mince pie), gingerbreads, and other forms of confectionery. France has a number of different fancy loaves and cakes. Some confections are especially associated with a particular locality. Thus Nuremberg has its *Lebkuchen*

or spice cakes, Aix-la-Chapelle its *Printen*, whilst Lubeck and Königsberg are famous for their marzipan—marzipan being, in fact, the German name for what in other countries, including Britain, was known as marchpane, a word of obscure origin denoting a paste of almonds and sugar moulded into ornamental shapes.

Gingerbreads were once very popular at Christmas time, and their use is frequently referred to in many countries. They were always made in a variety of forms—in the shape of men, animals, letters of the alphabet and so on. Often they were gilded. Shapes were specially made for the season in the image of Christmastide characters, such as St Nicholas. The making of gingerbreads goes back to the fifteenth century; there are those that say the making of these edible figurines originates in substitute dolls for human sacrifices—just as loaves in the shape of horns are claimed to represent sacrificial oxen.

Christmas, inevitably, is also celebrated by drinking. Wassailing is often mentioned in books about the 'old Christmas'. The word is of Anglo-Saxon origin, from *wes hal*, meaning 'be whole', or expressing a wish for good health. The wassail bowl, apart from the customs connected with it, was otherwise a beaker that was passed round at celebrations for the purpose of drinking toasts—its usual content being 'lambswool', which was hot spiced ale and toasted apples. Wassailing was applied, as will be seen later, to customs designed to bring fertility in agriculture. In fact, the toast seems often to imply some return, and was sometimes—like so many customs of the Twelve Days—little more than organized begging. In this case a free drink was the object, with dire consequences threatened if it were not forthcoming.

Under the Tudors and the Stuarts one of the chief entertainments of the Christmas season was the Church Ale, organized by the church-wardens as a means of raising money for church funds. Ale and food were sold in the Church House or a local barn, which had been specially decorated for the purpose—sometimes even in the church itself. Philip Stubbes, in his *Anatomie of Abuses*, 1583, inveighed against this regrettable practice:

> In certain townes, where dronken Bacchus beares swaie . . . the churchwardens of every parishe, with the consent of the whole parishe, provide halfe a score or twentie quarters of maulte, whereof some they buy of the church stocke, and some is given to them of the parishioners themselves, every one conferring somewhat, according to his abilitie; which maulte being made into very strong ale or bere, is sette to sale, either in the church or some other place assigned to that purpose. Then when this is set abroche, well is he that can gete the soonest to it, and spend the most at it.

John Nash, R.A. (b. 1893). Christmas card design. Printed by Lund, Humphries & Co. for the Poetry Bookshop, c. 1930.

Nineteenth-century Saturnalia. Mid-Victorian photograph.

5

Christmas Eve

Christmas Eve has never been part of the Feast of the Twelve Days. In the English-speaking world it is not specifically celebrated, except by the singing of carols and reading of lessons in King's College Chapel, Cambridge, by the excited anticipations of children everywhere, and by their parents leaving work early, having, perhaps, had rather more to drink at midday than is good for them, with much consequent manœuvring for position under the mistletoe.

On the Continent of Europe, however, there are many rituals, which in general take the form of variations on the St Nicholas theme, the saint being replaced by impersonators of other beings. In Germany there is the Christ Child, the *Christkind*—a strange mystical fairy-like creature often impersonated by a tall girl. Accompanying her, to admonish the wicked children, is the hideous Hans Trapp. Then there is Knecht Ruprecht, a weird figure concerned with the adequacy of praying and competency in catechisms. He was once held to be a descendant of Odin, but now he is said to be a creation of the seventeenth century.

Christmas Eve was also the occasion of the ceremonial bringing in of the Yule-log. We have it in Herrick:

> Come, bring with a noise,
> My merrie, merrie boyes,
> The Christmas Log to the firing;
> While my good Dame, she
> Bids ye all be free;
> And drink to your hearts desiring.
>
> With the last yeeres brand
> Light the new block, and

For good successe in his spending,
On your Psaltries play,
That sweet luck may
Come while the log is a-teending.

Drink now the strong Beere,
Cut the white loafe here,
The while the meat is a-shredding;
For the rare Mince-Pie
And the Plums stand by
To fill the paste that's a-kneading.

Today the bringing in of the Yule-log is an obsolete custom; indeed, more often than not, impracticable. Yet something of it survived when the Rev. Hilderic Friend wrote in 1883:

> Our Christmas ceremonies usually begin on Christmas Eve, when the Yule-log is burned. This old custom is fast dying out, but in Devonshire it is still observed. Often, in place of a log, a faggot is employed, and in the West of England the Ashen faggot is a regular institution. . . . The Ashen faggot was bound around with a number of bands or withes, and as each withe was burned asunder a new jug of cider was expected, the men who made up the faggot taking care to put as many bands around it as possible, to ensure a good supply of drink. The custom is still largely observed in many Devonshire villages and hamlets.

Traditionally the brands were saved and were used to relight the Christmas fire the following year. The customs and ceremonies associated with this now almost obsolete fire ceremony varied from country to country, but it once extended so far south as Northern Italy. The Rev. Hilderic Friend mentions the Christmas Eve *billet* which was common in France in mid-century. About six o'clock in the evening an immense log was placed on the fire, and the burning of it was believed to keep away pestilence from all seated around it. The custom was taken to America in its English version by colonists.

The burning of the Yule-log was sometimes supplemented or replaced by the burning of a candle on Christmas Day. 'I lighted my wax-candle being Xmas Day during Tea-time this afternoon for abt. an

Hour,' recorded Parson Woodforde in 1790. In 1841 R. T. Hampson wrote:

> In some places candles are made of a particular kind, because the candle that is lighted on Christmas Day must be so large as to burn from the time of its ignition to the close of the day, otherwise it will portend evil to the family for the ensuing year. The poor were wont to present the rich with wax tapers, and Yule candles are still in the north of Scotland given by merchants to their customers. At one time children at the village schools in Lancashire were required to bring each a mould candle before the *parting* or separation for the Christmas holidays.

Today the flames of the Saturnalian tapers are reflected in the electric candles on our Christmas trees, and the ancient festival of fire in the burning brandy which surrounds the Christmas pudding.

Christmas Eve has many supernatural associations which may be studied in books of folk-lore. It is often difficult to trace their connexion with the Christmas season as such. One of them is vividly recalled in a passage in *Hamlet*. It takes various forms, and is part of the complex folk-lore of cock-crow, the tradition being that Christ was born at cock-crow, and that before His birthday cocks crow the whole night through. Horatio and Marcellus are talking. The Ghost is present, and the crowing of a cock startles it. Marcellus observes that it 'faded on the crowing of the cock'. He continues with the legend:

> Some say that ever 'gainst that season comes
> Wherein our Saviour's birth is celebrated,
> The bird of dawning singeth all night long:
> And then, they say, no spirit dares stir abroad;
> The nights are wholesome; then no planets strike,
> No fairy takes, nor witch hath power to charm;
> So hallow'd and so gracious is the time.

Contrary to this was a belief held in many northern countries that wild, stormy spirits are abroad during the whole Twelve Days.

Christmas Eve, like the eve of several other feasts, is a great time for auguries (particularly for maidens to preview their husbands). And on

Christmas Eve the Scandinavian trolls (though rarely seen by man) feast, dance, and revel.

Probably the most widely held superstition is that between eleven and twelve on Christmas Eve and the first hour of Christmas Day the cattle kneel down in reverence, but any person who sees them dies within the year. This belief, which is clearly related to the traditional presence of cattle in the stable at Bethlehem, was held in parts of Wales well into the last century. Thomas Hardy knew of it, though apparently he was unaware of the ill consequences of eavesdropping:

> Christmas Eve, and twelve of the clock,
>   'Now they are all on their knees,'
> An elder said as we sat in a flock
>   By the embers in hearthside ease.
>
> We pictured the meek mild creatures where
>   They dwelt in their strawy pen,
> Nor did it occur to one of us there
>   To doubt they were kneeling then.
>
> So fair a fancy few would weave
>   In these years! Yet, I feel,
> If someone said on Christmas Eve,
>   'Come; see the oxen kneel
>
> 'In the lonely barton by yonder coomb
>   Our children used to know,'
> I should go with him in the gloom,
>   Hoping it might be so.

Some versions of the legend hold that the animals also speak. In Switzerland, it is recorded, one Christmas Eve a peasant crept into the stable where his oxen were quietly chewing the hay set before them. Soon after the peasant had hidden himself one of the oxen said to another, 'We are going to have a hard and heavy task to do this week.' 'How is that?' asked another of the oxen; 'The harvest is got in and we have drawn home all the winter fuel.' 'That is so,' was the reply, 'but we shall have to drag a coffin to the churchyard, for our poor master will most certainly die this week.' The peasant shrieked and fell back senseless. The ox's prophecy was fulfilled.

Cattle apart, there are many opportunities for wishful thinking or apprehensive terrors in the mythology of Christmas Eve. When the Yule-log burns, for instance, one should observe the shadows on the wall: those shadows that appear headless belong to people who will die within the year. If one puts a small heap of salt on the table on Christmas Eve and it melts during the night one will be dead in twelve months. If

Christmas Eve

it remains dry and undiminished one will live to a great age. And if a hoop falls off a cask on Christmas Eve some member of the household is sure to die before the following Christmas.

Spinsters may care to make the interesting experiment of pouring a ladleful of molten lead into cold water on Christmas Eve. When solidified, the lead will turn into the shape of the tools her future husband will use—a lancet-like shape if he is to be a doctor, a quill if he is to be a writer, a chain a surveyor, a mallet a mason, and so on.

Another traditional belief is that if wet straw-bands or hay-bands are tied round the trunks of fruit trees on Christmas Eve they will yield well in the ensuing year—not, presumably, an anticipation of the modern practice of grease-banding!

Until the latter part of the nineteenth century parties and games were a regular feature of Christmas Eve, especially the game called 'Snapdragon', which had been a familiar sport throughout the eighteenth century. Here is a description of 'Snapdragon' written as recently as the eighteen-eighties:

> A quantity of raisins are deposited in a large dish or bowl (the broader or shallower this is, the better), and brandy or some other spirit is poured over the fruit and ignited. The bystanders now endeavour, by turns, to grasp a raisin, by plunging their hands through the flames, and as this is somewhat of an arduous feat, requiring both courage and rapidity of action, a considerable amount of merriment is evoked at the expense of the unsuccessful competitors. Whilst the sport of Snapdragon is going on, it is usual to extinguish all the lights in the room, so that the lurid glare from the flaming spirits may exercise to the full its weirdlike effect.

As an accompaniment to this romantic but hazardous pastime the onlookers would sing this song:

> Here he comes with flaming bowl,
> Don't be mean to take his toll,
>   Snip! Snap! Dragon!
>
> Take care you don't take too much,
> Be not greedy in your clutch,
>   Snip! Snap! Dragon!
>
> With his blue and lapping tongue
> Many of you will be stung,
>   Snip! Snap! Dragon!
>
> For he snaps at all that comes
> Snatching at his feast of plums,
>   Snip! Snap! Dragon!

But Old Christmas makes him come,
Though he looks so fee! fa! fum!
  Snip! Snap! Dragon!

Don't 'ee fear him, be but bold—
Out he goes, his flames are cold.
  Snip! Snap! Dragon!

Today, all that remains of the traditional celebrations of the eve of Christmas is the hanging up of the children's stockings (or putting out their shoes), the decoration of the Christmas tree, and the strategic suspension of holly and mistletoe. The harassed housewife of today probably performs some of these tasks on Christmas Eve merely because she has not had time to do them earlier. Traditionally, however, it was considered extremely unlucky to bring holly or mistletoe into a house *before* Christmas Eve.

There is just one observance of Christmas Eve which, in country places in England at least, may possibly be gaining rather than losing ground. That is the ringing of church bells as summons to the midnight service—perhaps the most haunting and evocative expression of the significance of the Day that is to come; an echo, albeit halting and confused, of

Such musick (as 'tis said)
Before was never made,
But when of old the sons of morning sung . . .

6

St Nicholas and Santa Claus

Old Saint Nicholas comes so speedily
Over the frozen snow,
Lots of eatables, lots of drinkables,
Coming for me, I know . . .

So ran the first verse of a song which we sang in our childhood. It was printed in an old picture book—probably a translation from the German —opposite a vividly realistic illustration of the saint, spinning along in a heavily laden sledge, drawn by a team of reindeer.

Who was this gift-giving saint who, in his modern manifestation as Father Christmas or Santa Claus, dominates the modern mythology of Christmas Eve and Christmas Daybreak?

Very little is known of him. Nicholas of Patara was Bishop of Myra in Asia Minor during the fourth century. He was persecuted and imprisoned for his faith at the time of Diocletian, but he was not martyred. His piety had been shown in childhood, when he fasted regularly on Wednesdays and Fridays. On the early death of his father and mother he dedicated the rest of his life to the service of God. In pursuit of this he made a journey to Palestine, and in his voyaging he miraculously stilled a storm at sea. Hence, in Eastern Europe, Italy, and among the Greeks, he is patron of sailors. His feast is celebrated on the anniversary of his death, 6 December.

Elsewhere Saint Nicholas is held in repute for his generosity in saving the three daughters of a poor man from the life of shame to which he had condemned them because he could not afford dowries with which to endow husbands. Saint Nicholas presented each daughter with a bar of gold, and all was well. This action is charmingly recorded in one wing of a triptych painted by Gerard David (1460–1523) which

Thomas Nast (1840–1902). The modern prototype of Santa Claus.
Drawing for *Harper's Weekly*, c. 1865.

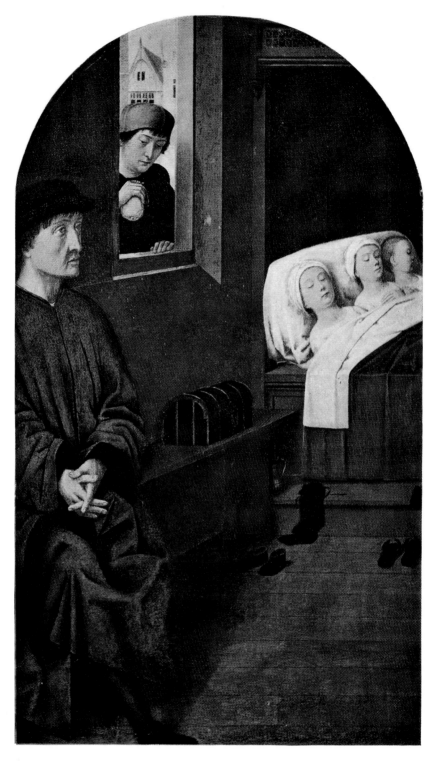

Gerard David (1450–1523). St Nicholas. Wing of a
triptych. *National Gallery of Scotland.*

shows the saint looking in through the window of the house where the poor man sits disconsolately contemplating the fate of the three daughters lying innocently a-bed. On account of this generous act St Nicholas is acknowledged in Southern Europe as the patron of maidens. H. D. Inglis, when visiting Alicante in Spain in December 1830, amusingly described his functions:

> The day after my arrival in Alicant chanced to be an important *dia de fiesta*; for it was no less than the patron Saint of the City (St Nicholas), who is besides the peculiar patron of all young women who wish to be married. In the evening I went to the cathedral, which was illuminated, and was filled with spectators; some seated upon mats, some standing: and in front of the altar an elevated plat-form was erected, upon which sat the Governor, and high civil and military officers. The Saint stood in a niche, in the centre of the altar, surrounded by lights; above, was an image of Christ, and below, an image of the Virgin. After the performance of some selections of music, all the female part of the audience pressed forward towards the Saint; for she who has the good fortune to see the Saint with his eyes open, will certainly be married the same year. There was much eagerness and much merriment among the ladies; and as I chanced to be in the current, I was carried in the same direction. I found that the merriment was owing to the difficulty of ascertaining what all were anxious to ascertain; for either the eyes of the Saint, or the lights, were so contrived, that it was impossible to determine whether his eyes were open or shut.

The feast of St Nicholas is, however, celebrated on its true day with greatest splendour in the majestic church of Bari, in south-eastern Italy, where his remains, allegedly stolen from Myra, now lie.

How is it that this patron of the seafarers and maidens of Mediter-ranean lands now appears with us in the north as St Nicholas with his reindeer, *alias* Santa Claus, *alias* Father Christmas, clambering down chimneys with a bag of presents, not on his proper day but on 24 December?

He seems to have emerged into St Nicholas as a gift-bearer on account of another miracle which accorded Nicholas high honour in the world of children. The story is that an innkeeper murdered three boys, and, to avoid detection, dismembered their bodies and soused them in a tub of pickle. Nicholas not only found their remains, but miraculously re-united the pieces to form the bodies, and restored the boys to life. Hence, he became the patron of children.

A rather vague but truly seasonal Father Christmas had long existed as a folk figure in the north of Europe. The Father Christmas who was

well known in medieval times—he appeared, for example, in the old mummers' plays—was quite a different figure from that which has been merged with the lore of St Nicholas. He was wholly pagan—more con-cerned with the adult significance of mistletoe and the Yule-log than with gifts for children. This view of him long persisted; it is shown as lately as 1848 in a poem illustrated and presumably written by 'Alfred Crowquill':

We know you ape the Christmas past,
 And totter in your gait:
But that bright sparkle in your eye
 Belies your bald old pate.
You take us in, you sly old rogue!
 You always like your joke:
You know you've got the mistletoe,
 In your capacious poke.

What have you got within that bowl,
 Of odour sweet and rare?
Is it a potion like the last,
 To wash away dull care?
To turn the heart from feud and gall,
 And drown the last year's strife—
And shattered circles join again,
 That should endure for life?

Then light the log of cheering blaze;
 We're waiting to a man
To sing the songs we've sung before,
 And pass the flowing can.
See how the smile and friendly grasp
 Are ready at your call,
And lips are waiting to be pressed—
 One heart shall be for all!

We know that you are not so old:
 You're full of youth and mirth.
Where is the robe of white, with which
 You mean to wed the earth?
We'll at your wedding dance i' faith—
 All friends so good and true—
And welcome in the young New Year,
 So quickly born of you.

The engraving that accompanies these rhymes shows a very different figure from the old gentleman we now see sitting in the stores, disguised in a red robe and white whiskers, distributing toys to the children after due prepayment.

This pagan Father Christmas can be seen in paintings by Jordaens, Metsu, Jan Steen, Greuze, and other artists, from the sixteenth century onwards. It has been suggested that he is descended from Saturn. His mutability until well past the middle of the last century can be observed in illustrations to periodicals or early Christmas cards. Amongst the illustrations, for example, in George Buday's *History of the Christmas Card* he sometimes takes the form of a small red-robed dwarf with a long-tailed hood of the Walt Disney school, sometimes of a majestic white-robed, white-bearded figure in a snow scene of Christmas trees (German). Not infrequently he is dressed in a green robe, with a holly or ivy wreath replacing the hood. In one of the cards reproduced by Mr Buday he is dressed in a short brown smock and carries a lute—an elderly Apollo pursuing an alarmed Victorian Daphne. It is not until we reach the eighteen-nineties that he becomes stereotyped as the conventional Santa Claus, bearing his heavy sack of toys.

There seems little doubt that we owe the present standardized figure to the United States, where St Nicholas, or in his less formal mode of address, Santa Claus, arrived in New York with the Dutch settlers in the seventeenth century.

This Dutch St Nicholas and his legend is well established by the realistic painters of the period. Jan Steen (1626–79), in a *genre* painting now in the Rijksmuseum at Amsterdam, reveals the whole story and its details. In the centre is the good little girl who has received her reward —a bucket full of toys, and, clutched in her hands, a Christ-child doll. Her now empty shoe lies in front. To the left is the bad boy, who, with his empty shoe, is being laughed at—the rod being at hand. The youngest children gaze up to the chimney whence the saint came. Also to be seen are sweets, many-shaped biscuits and gingerbreads, sometimes in the form of, or showing an image of St Nicholas: these were a feature of the day in several parts of Europe.

The gift-giving custom with which St Nicholas was concerned originally took place—and in some places still does—on the saint's properly appointed day, or its eve. It followed a form that is always basically the same but has many local variations. Nicholas appeared with, or his visit was presaged by, the arrival of an assistant—usually a hideous

Jan Steen (1626–79). St Nicholas's Day. *Rijksmuseum, Amsterdam.*

St Nicholas and St Fouettard. Nineteenth-century French broadside.

person, but sometimes even Christ, St Peter, an angel, or in Germany Knecht Ruprecht, the Christmas Eve figure. Inquiries are made about the behaviour of the little boys and girls in the household, whether they say their prayers, catechisms, and so on. St Nicholas rewards the good ones with gifts; the bad ones are duly punished.

A French 'strip' of the last century (*reproduced in part opposite*) well illustrates the general trend of the legend. On the eve of St Nicholas Maman hears a bell ringing down the street: *drelin, drelin, drelin*. . . . Excitedly she cries to her children: 'Entendez-vous la clochette de Saint Fouettard, le compagnon de Saint Nicolas? Il va venir pour savoir si vous avez étés bien sages: mettez-vous vite à genoux!'

In the next picture, with a courteous, 'Bonsoir, Madame,' St Fouettard enters—a loathsome-looking creature with a prodding nose, and armed, as his name implies, with whips and sticks. He announces that he is inquiring into the behaviour of the children on behalf of St Nicholas. As the result of his questioning, he hands bon-bons to the good (with a promise of more to come later from the saint) and rods to the bad. Before they go to bed, the children are instructed to place their shoes by the fireplace, and in them bouquets for St Nicholas and hay for his donkey; in the night he will come down the chimney.

Next we see Nicholas, accompanied by his informer. He is dressed not as the Santa Claus we know but as a bishop. St Fouettard leads a donkey which is laden with gifts. The saint announces that he will enter the home of the good little Marie, and give her 'bon-bons, des pralines, des pains d'épices [gingerbreads], des fruits confits, et puis un beau petit ménage'. In the fireplace he is delighted to find a posy of flowers for his feast-day and hay for the donkey.

In another picture, however, we see him at the home of a bad child, Auguste. Not only has he been warned by St Fouettard of Auguste's naughtiness, but the donkey refuses to eat the hay deceitfully set out to encourage a visit. Later, we see the good Nini with a doll and her brother crying 'Tra la la, quel bonheur!' with his beautiful Polichinelle. And, inevitably, the bad boy with the rod.

According to a correspondent to the *Illustrated London News* writing from France in 1849, this custom had been adapted to Christmas. The obnoxious St Fouettard, however, had disappeared in the process.

Having arrived with the Dutch in New York, St Nicholas behaved much as elsewhere, except that he required hay to be put out for a horse instead of a donkey. For long the legend was localized among those communities whose ancestors had brought it with them. In 1809 the Dutch story was repeated in Washington Irving's *Knickerbocker's History of New York*. This was widely read, and popularized St Nicholas throughout the States. Then, in 1823, was published a poem by a learned Hebrew scholar, Clement C. Moore (1779-1863), entitled 'A Visit from St Nicholas'. This we may regard, like Dickens's 'Christmas Carol', as one of the trust deeds of the modern Christmas:

'Twas the night before Christmas, when all through the house
Not a creature was stirring, not even a mouse . . .
The moon, on the breast of the new-fallen snow,
Gave a lustre of midday to objects below;
When what to my wondering eyes should appear,
But a miniature sleigh and eight tiny reindeer,
With a little old driver, so lively and quick
I knew in a moment it must be St Nick.
More rapid than eagles his coursers they came,
And he whistled and shouted and called them by name:
'Now, Dasher! now, Dancer! now, Prancer and Vixen!
On, Comet! on, Cupid! on, Donder and Blitzen!
To the top of the porch, to the top of the wall!
Now, dash away, dash away, dash away all!'
As dry leaves that before the wild hurricane fly,
When they meet with an obstacle, mount to the sky,
So, up to the house-top the coursers they flew,
With a sleigh full of toys—and St Nicholas too.
And then in a twinkling I heard on the roof
The prancing and pawing of each little hoof,
As I drew in my head and was turning around,
Down the chimney St Nicholas came with a bound.
He was dressed all in fur from his head to his foot,
And his clothes were all tarnished with ashes and soot;
A bundle of toys he had flung on his back,
And he looked like a pedlar just opening his pack,
His eyes how they twinkled! his dimples how merry!

His cheeks were like roses, his nose like a cherry;
His droll little mouth was drawn up like a bow,
And the beard on his chin was as white as the snow.
The stump of a pipe he held tight in his teeth,
And the smoke it encircled his head like a wreath.
He had a broad face, and a little round belly
That shook, when he laughed, like a bowl full of jelly.
He was chubby and plump—a right jolly old elf—
And I laughed when I saw him, in spite of myself.
A wink of his eye and a twist of his head
Soon gave me to know I had nothing to dread.
He spoke not a word, but went straight to his work,
And filled all the stockings; then turned with a jerk,
And laying his finger aside of his nose,
And giving a nod, up the chimney he rose.
He sprang to his sleigh, to his team gave a whistle,
And away they all flew like the down of a thistle;
But I heard him exclaim, ere he drove out of sight:
'Happy Christmas to all, and to all a good-night!'

This poem soon became immensely popular. It firmly established St Nicholas as a Christmas Eve figure throughout the North American continent, and projected him to a vast public as a traveller through the sky on a sleigh drawn by reindeer. Until the nineteenth century St Nicholas had travelled by horse, donkey, or in a sky-chariot pulled by horses (of various colours). He even had an aerial vehicle dragged by white goats. The reindeer-team is certainly an American invention—though to whom the credit is due is not quite apparent, for it is by no means certain that Moore's fancy was original.

Moore's St Nicholas, whom he also calls Santa Claus and St Nick, was an elfish figure. The credit for standardizing him visually in his present form is usually given to another American, Thomas Nast (1840–1902), the son of a musician in a Bavarian regiment who went to America. Nast was a vitriolic political cartoonist, but in 1863 he began a series of Christmas drawings in *Harper's Weekly*, which continued until 1886. During their course the appearance of his St Nicholas evolved into that of the Santa Claus we know today.

In 1897 a child wrote to the *New York Sun* asking if Santa Claus really existed, because her little friends said he did not. Francis Church, an editorial writer, produced a reply which was published at Christmas for the next fifty years:

> . . . Yes, Virginia, there is a Santa Claus. He exists as certainly as love and generosity and devotion exist, and you know that they abound and give to your life its highest beauty and joy. Alas! how dreary would be the world if there were no Santa Claus! It would be as dreary as if there were no Virginias. There would be no child-like faith then, no poetry, no romance to make tolerable this existence. We should have no enjoyment, except in sense and sight. The eternal light with which childhood fills the world would be extinguished.
>
> Not believe in Santa Claus! You might as well not believe in fairies! You might get your papa to hire men to watch in all the chimneys on Christmas Eve to catch Santa Claus, but even if they did not see Santa Claus coming down, what would that prove? Nobody sees Santa Claus, but that is no sign that there is no Santa Claus. The most real things in the world are those that no children or men can see. Did you ever see fairies dancing on the lawn? Of course not, but that's no proof that they are not there. Nobody can conceive all the wonders there are unseen or unseeable in the world. . . .
>
> No Santa Claus! Thank God! he lives, and he lives for ever. A thousand years from now, Virginia, nay, ten times ten thousand years from now, he will continue to make glad the heart of child-hood.

In 1914 the Santa Claus Association was formed by John D. Gluck of New York City 'to preserve children's faith in Santa Claus'. This was effected by obtaining from the Post Office the mail addressed to Santa Claus, and, when necessary, answering the letters and even sending presents.

The latest addition to the Santa Claus legend, his red-nosed reindeer Rudolph, arrived in 1939. Rudolph, of course, had a red nose that made him a joke and feel a failure in life. One Christmas Eve the night was so dark and overcast that Santa Claus could not find his way. Then Rudolph came into his own. His poor red nose glowed so brightly that he was put at the head of the reindeer team.

Rex Whistler (1905–44). Father Christmas. c. 1939.
By courtesy of Laurence Whistler, Esq. and The Wiggins Teape Group.

The Adoration of the Shepherds. Embroidered picture by Edmund
Harrison, Embroiderer to the King, 1637. *Victoria and Albert
Museum.*

7
Christmas Day

Wellcome, all WONDERS in one sight!
Aeternity shut in a span.
    Sommer in Winter, Day in Night.
Heaven in earth, & GOD in MAN.
    Great little one! whose all-embracing birth
Lifts earth to heaven, stoopes heav'n to earth.

    WELLCOME. Though nor to gold nor silk,
To more than Caesar's birth right is;
    Two sister-seas of Virgin-Milk,
With many a rarely-temper'd kisse
    That breathes at once both MAID & MOTHER,
Warmes in the one, cooles in the other.

    WELLCOME, though not to those gay flyes
Gilded i'th' Beames of earthly kings;
    Slippery soules in smiling eyes;
But to poor Shepheards, home-spun things:
    Whose Wealth's their flock; whose witt, to be
Well read in their simplicity.

    Yet when young April's husband showers
Shall blesse the fruitfull Maia's bed
    We'l bring the First-born of her flowers
To kisse thy FEET & crown thy HEAD.
    To thee, dread lamb! whose love must keep
The shepheards, more than they the sheep.

    To THEE, meek Majesty! soft KING
Of simple GRACES & sweet LOVES.
    Each of us his lamb will bring
Each his pair of sylver Doves;
    Till burnt at last in fire of Thy fair eyes,
Our selves become our own best SACRIFICE.

The foregoing verses from the chorus of Crashaw's 'Hymn Sung as by the Shepheards' remind us that the Nativity is the event to be celebrated on this day to the exclusion of all else; the pagan elements must recede and take their place in the Twelve Days that follow.

At an early stage, probably in the fifth century, the Church celebrated three Masses on Christmas Day, one at midnight, one at dawn, and one in full daylight. The Midnight Mass was singular to Christmas, as was the chanting of the *Gloria in excelsis*, the song of the angels. The later developments and variations in different Churches and countries are too numerous to recount. A not infrequent occurrence was that the congregation attending the Midnight Mass had been celebrating on Christmas Eve in an over-worldly manner and was noisy or even riotous. This seems to have been an incongruous continuation of the old pagan customs. At one time the Mass in Madrid was attended by crowds bringing tambourines and guitars, with which they accompanied the organ. The Mass ended, they danced within the church.

In parts of Germany, it seems, there was so much drunkenness that Midnight Mass was abandoned. In others, such as the Bavarian Highlands, the sight of the lantern-bearing peasants going to the village church, winding in and out of the banks of white snow like fireflies, has long been a scene lovingly described by poets, notably Rilke.

In most parts of Britain the Midnight Mass, or even a very early service, seems to have disappeared after the Reformation. Possibly it lingered longer than anywhere else in Wales. Marie Trevelyan wrote in her *Folk-lore and Folk-stories of Wales* (1909):

> The morning watch to celebrate the birth of Christ was known as the Plygain. This early service was held in all the parish churches in Wales at four o'clock in the morning of December 25th. It was continued until about the years 1850–56, and in some localities a few years later. The churches were brilliantly illuminated and beautifully decorated; a short service was held and carols were afterwards sung. It is singular to note that when the established Church discontinued Plygain, it was held in Nonconformist chapels, and the services were conducted with great fervour every year. The Wesleyan Methodists were among the last to celebrate the Plygain, which, translated, means the early morn or dawn.

In the Anglican Church, in the last few years, there has been a remarkable revival of the midnight service, with, alas, a corresponding diminution in the attendance at services on Christmas morning.

In the Greek Church Christmas is a lesser festival than Epiphany, and in Scotland and France the New Year is a more important secular celebration than Christmas. But Mme Th. Bentzen, recalling her childhood in France about the year 1850, gives a vivid picture of the Midnight Mass:

We started off, a number of us, together in a stream of light, which I called the glow-worm procession, over a road that at this nocturnal hour was not lacking in solemnity—the long avenue leading out from the park to the church. Our lanterns cast great shadows on the white road, crisp with frost which crackled under my feet as I walked. . . .

As our little group advanced, it saw others on the way, people from the farm and from the mill, who joined us, and, once on the Place de l'Église, we found ourselves with all the parishioners in a body. No one spoke—the icy north wind cut short our breath; but the voice of the chimes filled the silence. . . .

Above us the stars shone like diamond nails driven into velvet, and my eyes sought confidently the most beautiful, the one that guided the Wise Men, convinced as I was that it must guide us too, and all who are good. The old church, out of all proportion to the village of four hundred souls it sheltered, rose much more majestically than in the broad daylight; and how black was its ivy-mantled tower, which is all that remains to it from the thirteenth century! We entered, accompanied by a gust of wind that swept into the porch at the same time as we did; and the splendours of the altar, studded with lights, green with pine and laurel branches, dazzled us from the threshold. . . .

At once I looked for the *crèche*, the miniature stable, which we had been hard at work upon for at least a week, as the accessories from year to year needed repairing. The damaged animals had to be restored, the turbans and the cloaks of the Wise Men had to be made over, the straw freshened, and the figures that could no longer be used replaced by new effigies. It was a devout way of playing dolls; we went about it with a peculiar feeling of reverence.

And now the songs burst forth before the mass had even begun, the Christmas carols so old, so charming, sacred idylls in honour of Christ's nativity. . . .

I stayed awake determinedly, listening to those beloved refrains that one hears only at Christmas-time. I was less attentive to the sermon, a short one, however, on account of the late hour. It recalled simply to this rustic congregation the duty of giving alms in the name of him who, being God, was born destitute. This announced the moment for the collection.

Leaving part of my wrappings and my wooden shoes in the pew, I went about proudly, an embroidered red velvet bag in my hand, shaking it at every step to make the *sous* ring and clatter. But later it is very probable that sleep overcame me in spite of myself, for my mother had to rouse me when it was time to go, although the angels around us continued to sing endless *glorias*.

Every one went off to eat roast chestnuts soaked in the light white wine of the country, and we did like every one else, except that instead of this frugal repast it was a fat chicken or a turkey that awaited us. For dinner we had limited ourselves to a collation of *hors-d'oeuvres* and preserve in order to fast during our vigil and to enjoy our supper better after it; and what appetites! Hunger and cold got me wide awake on the way back. I enjoyed in anticipation the wonderful welcome that would greet us at home—gaiety, comfort, cheer and good food. At last we reached it all—a big fire where the Yule Log was burning, a well-laden table, a huge roast with its appetizing fumes, all sorts of luscious home-made pasties (we always sacrificed a pig at Christmas), and a sparkling wine from the neighbouring hillsides, which, in our opinion, was as good as the best champagne.

The gaieties of Christmastide were, in medieval England, unashamedly connected with the church, for the church was the natural centre of every parish. Wrestling and cock-fighting took place in church-yards, and dancing inside churches was not unknown. John Aubrey tells us that in his time, the second half of the seventeenth century, people in the north of England still danced in country churches after prayers at Christmas. 'And as they doe dance, they cry (or sing) Yole, Yole, Yole.'

Some curious instances of the place occupied by Christmas in the legal and social make-up of medieval England are to be found in Thomas Blount's *Antient Tenures of Land and Jocular Customs of some Mannors*, published in 1679. At Stamford,

> *William Earl Warren*, Lord of this Town in the time of King John, standing upon the Castle Walls, saw two Bulls fighting for a cow in the Castle Meadow, till all the Butchers Doggs pursued one of the Bulls (maddened with noise and multitude) clean through the Town. This sight so pleased the Earl, that he gave the Castle Meadow, where first the Bulls duel began, for a common to the Butchers of the Town, after the first Grass was mowed, on condition that they should find a mad Bull, the day six weeks before Christmas day, for the continuance of the sport for ever.

At Green's Norton, in Northamptonshire, the Green family had to lift up their right hands towards the king yearly on Christmas Day, wheresoever he should be in England. Other tenures were held by the presentation on Christmas Day of dishes of food, hens, robes, or other objects to the proprietor of the land. But certainly the most 'jocular' custom was at Hemingstone in Suffolk:

> Rowland Sarcere held one hundred and ten Acres of land in *Hemington* in Com. *Suffolk*, by Sergeanty for which on Christmas Day, every year before our Sovereign Lord the King of *England* he should perform *simul* & *semel*, unum *Saltum*, unum *Sufflum*, & unum *Bombulum*, or as we read elsewhere in French un saut, un pet, & un syflet, *simul* & *semel*; that is, he should dance, puff up his Cheeks, making therewith a sound, and let a Crack. *Et quia indecens servitium, ideo arrentatur** (sayes the Record).

Jocular customs originating in the Middle Ages continued throughout the Tudor and Stuart period. In a later chapter we shall mention some of the traditional Christmas entertainments of the past. Today, in Britain, Boxing Day is the occasion of a very full programme of professional football matches. In South Cardiganshire in the early nineteenth century, however, Christmas Day itself was celebrated by a game of football. The whole population of adjoining parishes, male and female,

* And because it is an indecent service, therefore it shall be rented.

participated. A writer in the *Oswestry Observer*, in 1887, recalls the custom as it was described to him by a man of eighty whom he met in Lampeter Workhouse:

> The parishioners of Celland and Pencarreg were particularly bitter in their conflicts; men threw off their coats and waistcoats, and women their gowns, and sometimes their petticoats. At Llanwennog, an extensive parish below Lampeter, the inhabitants for football purposes were divided into the Bros and the Blaenaus.... The Bros, it should be stated, occupied the high ground of the parish. They were nicknamed 'Paddy Bros' from a tradition that they were descendants from Irish people who settled on the hills in days long gone by. The Blaenaus occupied the lowlands, and, it may be presumed, were pure-bred Brythons. The more devout of the Bros and Blaenaus joined in the service at the parish church on Christmas morning. At any rate, the match did not begin until about midday, when the service was finished. Then the whole of the Bros and the Blaenaus, rich and poor, male and female, assembled on the turnpike road which divided the highlands from the lowlands. The ball . . . was thrown high in the air by a strong man, and when it fell Bros and Blaenaus scrambled for its possession, and a quarter of an hour frequently elapsed before the ball was got out from the struggling heap of human beings. Then if the Bros, by hook or by crook, could succeed in taking the ball up the mountain to their hamlet of Rhyddlan they won the day; while the Blaenaus were successful if they got the ball to their end of the parish at New Court. The whole parish was the field of operations, and sometimes it would be dark before either party scored a victory. . . . When once the goal was reached, the victory was celebrated by loud hurrahs and the firing of guns.

In our less robust and rumbustious civilization, after church service and present giving and a heavy midday dinner, Christmas Day tends to be rather quiet and dozy. Families are reunited—perhaps for this one day in the year, and they tend to sit and talk and relax.

A surprising and imaginative innovation was introduced to a much more extensive family by King George V on Christmas Day 1932. Through millions of radio sets his harsh but homely voice was heard— by many for the first time:

Through one of the marvels of modern science I am enabled this Christmas Day to speak to all my peoples throughout the Empire. I take it as a good omen that wireless should have reached its present perfection at a time when the Empire has been linked in closer union, for it offers us immense possibilities to make that union closer still. . . .

The perpetuation of this custom by his son and his grand-daughter has indeed carried the Christmas conception of family reunion into the wider context of a family of free nations, owing only an emotional allegiance to its head. That this is an entirely logical expression of the Christmas message, as well as one of sentiment, is evident if we turn our thoughts again to those who were personally concerned in the first Christmas of all; they too were a family. There is no mother who cannot share and understand the feelings expressed by Francis Quarles some three hundred years ago:

> O! What a ravishment 't had been, to see
> Thy little *Saviour* perking on thy *Knee*!
> To see him nuzzle in thy Virgin-Breast:
> His milk-white body all unclad, undrest!
> To see thy busie fingers cloathe and wrap
> His spreading limbs in thy indulgent Lap!
> To see his desp'rate *Eyes*, with Childish grace,
> Smiling upon his smiling Mother's face!

8

Carols and Christmas Songs

The early Roman Church had its Christmas hymns—in Latin, of course. Some of them survive and are still in use. But they were theological in matter, and, because of their language, ecclesiastical in manner and remote from the great mass of the people. To the people, Christmastide was much more than a religious observance—it was a still-living memory of pagan customs, of feasting and other good things of life. For them, in due course, was evolved a series of songs in the vernacular —often with elements of the good old customs remaining in them— but essentially a popularization of the true Christmas theme.

The word 'carol' is of French origin, meaning originally a ring dance accompanied by singing. By the beginning of the sixteenth century it had come to mean more especially a song of joy sung at Christmas in celebration of the Nativity. Subsequently the word was applied in a much lesser degree to songs sung at Easter and on similar occasions. It is important to remember this connexion between carols and the common people rather than any of the established Churches—which, indeed, have for long periods frowned upon them.

The popularization of the Christian faith was largely advanced—as we have seen in the case of the *presèpio*—by the early Franciscans. And it was one of that order, the Blessed Jacopone of Todi, who first produced Christian songs in the tongue of the common people instead of the scholar's Latin.

This saint was born into a good family at Todi in Umbria about the year 1230. He married a beautiful and virtuous wife, who was killed after only a year of blissful marriage. She was present at a wedding *festa* when a balcony on which she was standing collapsed; she was the only one killed in the disaster. This wrought a remarkable change in

Angel Musician. Stained glass roundel, from Hardwicke House,
Bury St Edmunds, c. 1400. *Victoria and Albert Museum.*

The Adoration of the Magi and Shepherds. French miniature painting from a Book of Hours of Margaret of Foix, c. 1480. (Actual size.)
Victoria and Albert Museum.

Jacopone. He became a Franciscan of overpowering faith, a kind of Christian Diogenes. He was often at loggerheads with his brethren, to whom the mortifications of the flesh to which he subjected himself from time to time made him a most uncongenial companion. His self-abasement has been described as eccentricity by some, as madness by others. Jacopone died on Christmas Day 1306.

Such was the man who has been described as producing 'the first real outburst of Christmas joy in a popular tongue'. John Addington Symonds, in *The Renaissance in Italy*, calls him 'the man who struck the key-note in religious popular poetry'. Symonds translated some of his poems, such as *Il Presèpio* (The Manger), of which the following is an extract:

> Come and look upon her child.
> Nestling in the hay!
> See his fair arms opened wide,
> On her lap to play!
> And she tucks him by her side,
> Cloaks him as she may:
> Gives her paps unto his mouth,
> Where his lips are laid.
>
> For the little babe had drouth,
> Sucked the breast she gave;
> All he sought was that sweet breast,
> Broth he did not crave;
> With his tiny mouth he pressed
> Tiny mouth that clave:
> Ah, the tiny baby thing,
> Mouth to bossom laid!
>
> Little angels all around
> Danced, and carols flung;
> Making verselets sweet and true,
> Still of love they sung;
> Calling saints and sinners too
> With love's tender tongue;
> Now that heaven's high glory is
> On this earth displayed . . .

In Germany during the fourteenth century there was a similar popularization of Christianity, whose driving force was the Dominican Order. To this we owe that most famous of carols, *In Dulci Jubilo*. One day the mystic Heinrich Suso was comforted in his sufferings by the arrival of a band of angels. They took him by the hand and led him to dance. One began a glad song about the child Jesus—the words of which were part in German, part in Latin. We may perhaps savour its qualities best in a Scots translation of 1567:

> *In dulci Jubilo*, Now lat us sing with myrth and jo
> Our hartis consolatioun lyis *in praesipio*,
> And schynis as the Sone, *Matris in gremio*,
> *Alpha es et O, Alpha es et O.*
> *O Jesu parvule!* I, thrist sore efter thé
> Confort my hart and mynde, *O puer optime*,
> God of all grace sa kynde, *et princeps gloriae*
> *Trahe me post te, Trahe me post te.*
> *Ubi sunt gaudia*, in ony place bot thair,
> Quhair that the Angellis sing *Nova cantica*,
> Bot and the bellis ring *Nova cantica, in regia cantica curia*,
> God gif I war thair, God gif I war thair.

In Britain the first of the popularizers was John Audelay. He was probably a chantry priest of Lord Strange of Knockin, a village in Shropshire not far from the Augustinian Abbey of Haughmond. He wrote of himself as 'ye synful Audelay' and 'Mi name hit is ye blind Awdlay'. At Haughmond he produced a small number of poems, presumably in old age, which includes a section headed 'Syng these Caroles in Cristmas'. Today, unfortunately, they are practically unintelligible except to the scholar, and we cannot find a translation into modern English.

The medieval plays also contained verses of a carol-like nature. There is a song of this kind in a Coventry Corpus Christi pageant:

> As I out rode this enderes night,
> Of three joli sheppardes I saw a sight,
> And all about there fold a star shone bright.
>   They sange 'Terli terlow'.
> So mereli the sheppards their pipes can blow.

Doune from heaven, from heaven so hie,
Of angeles ther came a great companie,
With mirthe and joy and great solemnitye,
    They sang 'Terli terlow'.
So mereli the sheppards their pipes can blow.

The French Christmas song, the *Noël*, was rather later in development. In general it is more personal, and with much vivid local detail. Many were popular, even coarse and vulgar songs, turned into 'good and godly ballads'.

Returning to England, we find a representative collection of carols in Richard Hill's manuscript commonplace book, owned by Balliol College, Oxford. We may take a few representative verses to indicate the principal types. First, there is the triumphant song:

A babe is born, to blys vs brynge.
I hard a mayd lulley & synge;
She said: 'Dere son, leave thy wepyng,
    Thy fader is ye kyng of blis.'
        Now sing we with angelis:
        Gloria in excelsis!

Then there are those of welcome and joyful salutation:

In to this world, this day dide com
Jhesu Criste, both God & man,
Lord and servant, in on person,
    Born of ye blessid virgyn Mary.
        I pray you, be merry and synge with me
        In worship of Cristys nativitie.

There are the gentle lullaby carols:

So bless'd a sight it was to see
How Mary rokked her son so fre!
So frayre she rokked & songe 'by, by';
    Myn own dere moder, syng lulley!
        Lulley, Jhesu, lulley, lulley!
    Myn own dere moder, syng lulley.

And the even more beautiful:

> A lovely lady sat & songe
> And to her son thus gan she say:
> 'My son, my lord, my dere derlyng,
> Why liggis thou thus in hay?
>> Myn own dere son,
>> How art thou cum,
>>> Art thou not God verrey?
>> But never the lesse
>> I will not sees
>>> To syng "by, by, lulley, lulley".'

> This enders nyght
> I sawe a sight,
> A sterre as bryght
>> As any day;
> & euer a-monge,
> A maydyn songe:
>> 'Lulley, by, by, lulley!'

Elizabethan swagger and grandeur is very evident in this verse from one of William Byrd's *Songs of Sundrie Natures*, published in 1589:

> O sing unto this glittering, glorious King,
>> O praise his name let every living thing;
> Let heart and voice like bells of silver ring
>> The comfort that this day to man doth bring:
> Let lute, let shawm, with sound of sweet delight
>> These joys of Christ His birth this day recite.
>>> Rejoice, rejoice, with heart and voice,
>>> In Christ His birth this day rejoice.

The lullaby style, now with a typical new Elizabethan twist to the idea, is demonstrated in another of Byrd's carols from the same collection:

> Then let us sing the lullabies of sleep
>> To this sweet Babe, born to awake us all
> From drowsy sin that made old Adam weep,
>> And by his fault gave to mankind a fall.

For lo! this birth-day, day of days,
Summons our songs, to give him laud and praise.
Cast off all doubtful care,
Exile and banish tears,
To joyful news divine
Lend us your list'ning ears.

The vernacular nature of the carol is emphasized by the inclusion of 'The Cherry Tree Carol' in J. E. Housman's *British Popular Ballads*. He tells us that this ballad-carol derives its strange story from the Apocryphal Gospel of Pseudo-Matthew. No text earlier than the eighteenth century survives, but the ballad is assumed to go back to a much earlier period. It shows how an old legend from an inaccessible source can survive in the popular mind:

Joseph was an old man,
and an old man was he,
When he wedded Mary,
in the land of Galilee.

Joseph and Mary walked
through an orchard good,
Where was cherries and berries,
so red as any blood.

Joseph and Mary walked
through an orchard green,
Where was berries and cherries,
as thick as might be seen.

O then bespoke Mary,
so meek and so mild:
'Pluck me one cherry, Joseph,
for I am with child.'

O then bespoke Joseph,
with words most unkind:
'Let him pluck thee a cherry
that brought thee with child.'

F

O then bespoke the babe
    within his mother's womb;
'Bow down then the tallest tree,
    for my mother to have some.'

Then bowed down the highest tree
    unto his mother's hand;
Then she cried, 'See, Joseph,
    I have cherries at command.'

O then bespoke Joseph:
    'I have done Mary wrong;
But cheer up, my dearest,
    and be not cast down.'

Then Mary plucked a cherry,
    as red as the blood,
Then Mary went home
    With her heavy load.

Then Mary took her babe,
    and sat him on her knee,
Saying, 'My dear son, tell me,
    what this world will be.'

'O I shall be as dead, mother,
    as the stones in the wall;
O the stones in the streets, mother,
    shall mourn for me all.

'Upon Easter day, mother,
    my uprising shall be;
O the sun and the moon, mother,
    shall both rise with me.'

*   *   *

The Reformation discouraged carols, though in Germany something of their feeling was carried on in the Protestant Christmas hymns. In Britain we suffered the Puritans, and though we had such Christmas poets as Herrick and Wither, they were not true carollers. In France, at a rather later date, the Revolution largely ended the *Noëls*.

Parson Woodforde in 1781 gave 6d. to 'Spragg's lame son for a Christmas Carol'. But his parishioners did not sing them in church: it was the malformed boy of the common people who kept the carol alive. By the beginning of the nineteenth century carols were a thing of the past. Antiquarians sought them out in remote corners of Britain. One of the first to describe the curious old-world practice of carol singing was William Hone in his book significantly called *Ancient Mysteries Described* (1823):

> The custom of singing carols at Christmas prevails in Ireland to the present time. In Scotland where no church feasts have been kept since the days of John Knox, the custom is unknown. In Wales it is still preserved to a greater extent, perhaps, than in England; at a former period, the Welsh had carols adapted to most of the ecclesiastical festivals, and the four seasons of the year, but at this time they are limited to that of Christmas. After the turn of midnight at Christmas eve, service is performed in the churches, followed by singing of carols to the harp. Whilst the Christmas holidays continue, they are sung in like manner in the houses, and there are carols specially adapted to be sung at the doors of the houses by visitors before they enter. *Lffyr Carolan*, or the Book of Carols, contains sixty-six for Christmas, and five summer carols; *Blodeugerrd Cymrii*, or the Anthology of Wales, contains forty-eight Christmas carols, nine summer carols, three May carols, one winter carol, one nightingale carol, and a carol to Cupid. The following verse of a carol for Christmas is literally translated from the first-mentioned volume. The poem was written by Hugh Morris, a celebrated song-writer during the Commonwealth. . . .
>
> > *To a saint let us not pray, to a pope let us not kneel;*
> > *On Jesu let us depend, and let us discreetly watch*
> > *To preserve our souls from Satan with his snares;*
> > *Let us not in a morning invoke any one else.*

There is no mention of English carols. Hone accepted the fact that carol singing was, if not quite dead, dying—an 'ancient mystery'.

Almost concurrently Davies Gilbert published in 1822 his small *Collection of Christmas Carols*. Gilbert was a remarkable man, as much interested in forgotten things of the past as in the inventions of Humphry

Davy, the engineering achievements of Brunel, and the activities of the Royal Society, of which he was President. His book was successful and was reprinted.

Then came the solicitor-antiquary, William Sandys, in 1833 with his fine book, *Christmas Carols, Ancient and Modern; including the Most Popular in the West of England, and the Airs to Which They are Sung.* He added some French carols, and excellent notes. Sandys, like the other antiquaries, despaired of the survival of the carol:

> In the metropolis a solitary itinerant may be occasionally heard in the streets, croaking out 'God rest you merry, gentlemen,' or some other old carol, to an ancient and simple tune. Indeed, many carols are yet printed in London for the chapmen, or dealers in cheap literature; and I have some scores of half-penny and penny carols of this description. . . . Several of these carols have woodcuts of the rudest description; others again have embellishment that might have been considered very creditable for the price at which they are afforded, until recent examples had shown us the extent of ornament which may be lavished even on a penny publication. Some of these carols, I was informed by the publishers, are in considerable request, and are printed off as the demand requires. The custom prevails also in Ireland and Wales. In the latter country in particular, there are several collections known in the Welsh language; some of which are of ancient date. Others are composed by the modern village-poet. . . . There was a notice recently of the death of a Welsh poet, David Jones, at Rhuddlan, in Flintshire, aged sixty-nine, who for the last fifty-three years had annually sung a carol, of his own composing, on Christmas Day, in the church there.

Sandys reprinted seventy-five songs, some of which were scarcely Christmas carols in the modern sense. To these he added six French *Noëls*. He included eighteen tunes, which included those of 'The First Nowell', 'God Rest you Merry, Gentlemen', 'To Morrow Shall Be My Dancing Day' and 'I Saw Three Ships'. He found it necessary to remark of these tunes—today familiar to everyone—that they are 'of a pleasing and plaintive nature, and most of them appear to be of considerable antiquity'.

'The Christmas Waits'. Lithographic music cover for Comic Quadrille by Henri Laurent, c. 1860.

'Phiz' (Hablot K. Browne, 1815–82). A Christmas Carol. Coloured
engraving. 1858.

In the meantime the popular ballad element of Christmas song was being revived. In Austria 'Silent Night' was composed in 1818. At Hallein in the Tyrol (so it is said) Father Joseph Mohr had been so impressed by the sight of his parishioners coming on Christmas Eve to the Midnight Mass that after the Mass he sat down and composed a poem on the subject. During the night mice nibbled the works of the old organ and it was silenced. In order that there should be music Franz Gruber, the local schoolmaster and organist, composed a tune on his guitar to accompany Father Mohr's new poem. It remained merely a local song until heard by an organ-mender, who wrote it down for the daughters of one Strasser to sing. Through them it came to the ears of the Director-General of Music in Saxony, thence to the world. Franz Gruber's guitar is still preserved and exhibited.

Nor should we forget the English romantic ballad writers who kept popular Christmas music alive. Almost unknown to younger generations, except for the story, is the ballad of 'The Mistletoe Bough'. But those whose memories go back to the last days of the itinerant Christmas waits will remember the crunching of the gravel as the bandsmen took up their stances, adjusted their cornets and euphoniums and led off with Sir Henry Bishop's booming tune.

The author, Thomas Haynes Bayly (1797–1839), was the son of a Bath solicitor and lived a short, and financially unfortunate, life. After abandoning the law and the Church, he took to writing ballads and plays. Many of the songs he wrote are sentimental trifles of the drawing-room. But 'The Mistletoe Bough' is the stuff of legend:

> The mistletoe hung in the castle hall,
> The holly branch shone on the old oak wall;
> And the baron's retainers were bright and gay,
> And keeping their Christmas holiday.
> The baron beheld, with a father's pride,
> His beautiful child, young Lovell's bride;
> While she, with her bright eyes, seem'd to be
> The star of the goodly company.
> > Oh! the mistletoe bough!
> > Oh! the mistletoe bough!

'I'm weary of dancing now,' she cried;
'Here tarry a moment—I'll hide—I'll hide.
And Lovell, be sure thou'rt first to trace
The clue to my secret lurking place.'
Away she ran—and her friends began
Each tower to search, and each nook to scan;
And young Lovell cried, 'Oh! where dost thou hide?
I'm lonesome without thee, my own dear bride.'
    Oh! the mistletoe bough! *etc.*

They sought her that night! and they sought her next day!
And they sought her in vain, when a week pass'd away!
In the highest—the lowest—the loneliest spot
Young Lovell sought wildly—but found her not.
And years flew by, and their grief at last
Was told as a sorrowful tale long past;
And when Lovell appear'd the children cried,
'See! the old man weeps for his fairy bride.'
    Oh! the mistletoe bough! *etc.*

At length an oak chest, that had long lain hid
Was found in the castle—they raised the lid—
And a skeleton form lay mouldering there,
In the bridal wreaths of that lady fair!
Oh! sad was her fate!—in sportive jest
She hid from her lord in the old oak chest,
It closed with a spring!—and, dreadful doom,
The bride lay clasp'd in her living tomb!
    Oh! the mistletoe bough! *etc.*

As children, duly impressed by the awful solemnity and detailed realism of this ballad, we were given various and conflicting accounts of the origin of the legend: that it actually occurred at Marwell Hall, at Owlesbury, near Winchester—at the palace-like Bramshill in Hampshire—at the grey stone Cotswold manor of Minster Lovell. But Bayly quoted at the head of his ballad lines from *Ginevra*, a poem by Samuel Rogers, which relates the same tale about a lady's fate after her betrothal to Francesco Doria of Medina. The mistletoe and the English setting were Bayly's local colour.

Whilst Bayly's tragic ballad was riding to popularity on the revival of

the 'olde-worlde' Christmas in early Victorian times, the forebodings of
Sandys about the carol were to prove wrong. A landmark was the publication in 1853 of *Carols for Christmastide*. This was the production of the
Rev. John Mason Neale (1818–66), who was responsible for the literary
matter, and the Rev. Thomas Holman Helmore (1811–90), a musician.

This little collection was important for two reasons. Neale had obtained through the British Minister at Stockholm a copy of *Piae
Cantiones*, a collection of religious songs compiled by Theodoricus
Petrus of Nyland, Finland, in 1582. This contained some of what are
now our best-known tunes. Neale handed it to Helmore to arrange the
music, while he wrote new words, sometimes based on old verses, to
match them.

The discovery of the *Cantiones* was important enough, but the publication of Neale's collection was notable for another reason. One of the
songs that Neale wrote for the music was 'Good King Wenceslas'.
Now variously described as doggerel and a poor example of the pseudo-
Gothic romantic ballad, 'Good King Wenceslas', by the immense swing
of the march-like tune and the simple moral of the story, maintains an
unchallenged position as the most popular carol of all. It possesses, above
all, the essential quality of a carol: it is a song of the people, who kept the
form alive when educated persons would have let it die.

It seems that Neale took the story from a medieval Latin legend.
It might relate to the Bohemian King and saint, Vaclav—though there
is no native tradition to support it. He was murdered by his heathen
brother in 935, having previously founded the cathedral of St Vitus, the
resting-place of Bohemian kings. The story only became known in
Vaclav's own country through a translation of Neale's carol into Czech.

Even the success of Neale's and Helmore's work did not firmly re-
establish the carol among church congregations. This was effected from
1871 onwards. In that year was published the first of several editions of
Christmas Carols New and Old, the words edited by the Rev. Henry
Ramsden Bramley, the music by Dr John Stainer, 'both of the St Mary
Magdalen College, Oxford'. This collection contained forty-two carols.
Subsequent editions increased the number to seventy, each of which was
obtainable separately at one penny. This publication was immensely

successful and became widely used in churches.* Some of the carols were alas, feeble stuff, though the composers of the new tunes included Sullivan, Ousely, Bridge, and Goss.

The final stage was the revival of folk music led by such men as Cecil Sharp, Vaughan Williams, Percy Dearmer, and Martin Shaw. The last three were responsible for the *Oxford Book of Carols*, with words and music of over two hundred carols, published in 1928. This is a scholarly and well-annotated collection, but in its way is as much of a period piece as Bramley's and Stainer's. It tends to lack the vulgar vigour and sweet sentimentality of the common people which is so essential to the carol.

In other European countries the revival followed something of the same lines. In France, for example, there was Father Pérennès' volume in the *Encyclopédie Théologique*, the *Dictionnaire de Noëls et de Cantiques*, a vast collection, published in 1867, containing words and tunes.

A survey of carols would be incomplete if mention were not made of some examples written by poets, rather than songsters, during the last century, some of which have not achieved musical settings. Such was the remarkable 'King Arthur's Waes-Hael' written by the Rev. Robert Stephen Hawker (1804–75). Hawker was a Cornish parson, of an antiquarian turn of mind, interested in revivals of old customs, such as the harvest festival:

> Waes-hael for knight and dame!
>   O merry be their dole!
> Drink-hael! in Jesu's name
>   We fill the tawny bowl;
> But cover down the curving crest,
> Mould of the Orient Lady's breast.
>
> Waes-hael! yet lift no lid:
>   Drain ye the reeds for wine.
> Drink-hael! the milk was hid
>   That soothed that Babe divine;
> Hush'd, as this hollow channel flows,
> He drew the balsam from the rose.

* For example, on 25 December 1880, the Vicar of East Dereham, Norfolk, noted that carols were first introduced into the service.

Waes-hael! thus glow'd the breast
　　Where a God yearn'd to cling;
Drink-hael. So Jesu press'd
　　Life from its mystic spring;
Then hush and bend in reverent sign
And breathe the thrilling reeds for wine.

Waes-hael! in shadowy scene
　　Lo! Christmas children we:
Drink-hael! behold we lean
　　At a far mother's knee;
To dream that thus her bosom smiled,
And learn the lip of Bethlehem's child.

The Pre-Raphaelites, in their own odd way, were deeply interested in the Nativity. (There is Sir Edward Burne-Jones's huge picture, 'The Star of Bethlehem'.) Christina Rossetti (1830–94) wrote more than one Christmas poem, particularly 'In the Bleak Mid Winter', whose purity and simplicity of feeling and phrase should put it among the traditional favourites. Though it has in fact been set to music it is surprisingly seldom sung.

Christina Rossetti's brother, Dante Gabriel, made a drawing which resulted in a rather surprising Christmas Carol from Swinburne:

Three damsels in the queen's chamber,
　　The queen's mouth was most fair;
She spake a word of God's mother
　　As the combs went in her hair.
　　　　Mary that is of might,
　　　　Bring us to thy Son's sight.

They held the gold combs out from her,
　　A span's length off her head;
She sang this song of God's mother
　　And of her bearing-bed.
　　　　Mary most full of grace,
　　　　Bring us to thy Son's face.

When she sat at Joseph's hand
    She looked against her side;
And either way from the short silk band
    Her girdle was all wried.
        Mary that all good may,
        Bring us to thy Son's way.

Mary had three women for her bed.
    The twain were maidens clean;
The first of them had white and red,
    The third had riven green.
        Mary that is so sweet,
        Bring us to thy Son's feet.

She had three women for her hair,
    Two were gloved soft and shod;
The third had feet and fingers bare.
    She was the likest God.
        Mary that wieldeth land,
        Bring us to thy Son's hand.

She had three women for her ease.
    The twain were good women.
The first two were the two Maries,
    The third was Magdalen.
        Mary that perfect is,
        Bring us to thy Son's kiss.

Joseph had three workmen in his stall,
    To serve him well upon;
The first of them were Peter and Paul,
    The third of them was John.
        Mary, God's handmaiden,
        Bring us to thy Son's ken.

'If your child be none other man's,
    But if it be very mine,
The bedstead shall be gold two spans,
    The bedfoot silver fine.'
        Mary that made God mirth,
        Bring us to thy Son's birth.

'If the child be some other man's,
    And if it be none of mine,
The manger shall be straw two spans,
    Betwixen kine and kine.'
        Mary that made sin cease,
        Bring us to thy Son's peace.

Christ was born upon this wise,
    It fell on such a night,
Neither with sounds of psalteries,
    Nor with fire for light.
        Mary that is God's spouse,
        Bring us to thy Son's house.

The star came out upon the east
    With a great sound and sweet:
Kings gave gold to make him feast
    And myrrh for him to eat.
        Mary, of thy sweet mood,
        Bring us to thy Son's good.

He had two handmaids at his head,
    One handmaid at his feet;
The twain of them were fair and red,
    The third one was right sweet.
        Mary that is most wise,
        Bring us to thy Son's eyes.

In the twentieth century some profound and eloquent poems have been written about Christmas—by Hardy, by Chesterton, by Belloc, Walter de la Mare, Robert Frost, T. S. Eliot, Allen Tate, and others. But it is difficult to think of many that have that simplicity of theme and directness of utterance which makes a carol for the people. Nonetheless there seems to us an opportunity for some musician with an ear for folk music—Mr Benjamin Britten, for instance—to add a twentieth-century carol to the popular canon. For the words he might consider these by a living Irish poet, W. R. Rodgers:

Deep in the fading leaves of night
There lay the flower that darkness knows,
Till winter stripped and brought to light
The most incomparable Rose
That blows, that blows.

The flashing mirrors of the snow
Keep turning and returning still:
To see the lovely child below
And hold him is their only will;
Keep still, keep still.

And to let go his very cry
The clinging echoes are so slow
That still his wail they multiply
Though he lie singing now below,
So low, so low.

Even the doves forget to grieve
And gravely to his greetings fly
And the lone places that they leave
All follow and are standing by
On high, on high.

The Wilton Diptych: the right wing. French School. c. 1395.
National Gallery.

George Cruikshank (1792–1878). Christmas Revels. Engraving.

9

Christmas Remembered

What we have written so far forms little more than the skeletal branches of the Christmas tradition. The time has come to deck the tree with candles of personal recollection whose glimmering rays may express some of the transient sensations and sentiments, the undertones and overtones, of Christmas as it has been celebrated through the years. If the effect is at times inconsequent and bizarre—well, that is in the spirit of the season.

> Little Jack Horner
> Sat in a corner
> Eating his Christmas pie.
> He put in his thumb
> And pulled out a plum,
> And said, what a good boy am I.

The traditional legend behind this exceedingly brief Christmas anecdote is that at the time when Henry VIII was seizing the monasteries the Abbot of Glastonbury hoped by a tactful gesture to appease his sovereign. He had a Christmas pie baked wherein he concealed the title deeds of several of his manors. This unusually rich confection he despatched to the King in charge of his steward, a man named Horner. During the journey, however, the astute Horner abstracted the title to the manor of Mells in Somerset and retained it for himself. His descendants who occupy the place strongly deny this story, and rather curiously the rhyme did not find its way into print until early in the last century. But there is a rhyme, presumably of some age when it was first printed in 1688, which relates that:

> Hopton, Horner, Smyth and Thynne,
> When abbots went out, they came in.

The merrymaking of the Christmas season, as we have seen, goes back far into the Middle Ages; so does the supervision of the festivities by a Lord of Misrule. John Stow describes the procedure in his *Survey of London* (1598):

> There was in the king's house, wheresoever he was lodged, a lord of misrule, or master of merry disportes, and the like had ye in the house of every nobleman of honour. . . . Amongst the which the mayor of London, and either of the sheriffs, had their several lords of misrule, ever contending, without quarrel or offence, who should make the rarest pastimes to delighte the behoulders. These lords beginning their rule on Alhalloud Eve, continued the same till the morrow after the Feast of the Purification, commonly called Candlemas day. In all which space there were fine and subtil disguisinges, masks and mummeries, with playing at cards for counters, nayles and points, in every house, more for pastime than for gaine.

At Oxford and Cambridge there were Lords of Misrule in the colleges; Lincoln's Inn appointed a King of Christmas. All had freedom to do as they pleased during the Christmas season, and considerable funds were put at their disposal. The accounts of Henry VII record a payment in 1490 of £32 18*s*. 6½*d*. to Jacques Haulte for 'the disguising'. A contemporary view of the Court festivities in 1603 is given in the journal of Sir Roger Wilbraham:

> The first *Christmas* of worthy king James was at his court at Hampton, Ao. 1603: wher the French, Spanish & Polonian Ambassadors were severallie solemplie feasted: name plaies & daunces with swordes: one mask by English and Scottish lords: another by the Queen's Maiestie & eleven more ladies of her chamber presenting giftes as goddesses. The maskes, especialli the laste, costes 2000l. or 3000l. the apparells: rare musick, fine songes: & in jewels most riche 20000l., the lest to my iudgment: & her maiestie 10000l. after Christmas was running at Ring by the King & 8 or 9 lords for the honour of those goddesses & then they all feasted together privatelie.

There were Lords of Misrule at the Court of Charles I, and John Evelyn's father drew up 'articles' appointing one for his own household, with complete authority for the whole season. Under the Commonwealth, however, the Puritans put an end not merely to such levities but also to Christmas itself. The *Flying Eagle*, of 24 December 1652, reported thus on transactions in Parliament:

> The House spent much Time this Day about the businesse of the Navie, for settling the Affairs at Sea, and before they rose, were presented with a terrible Remonstrance against Christmas-day, grounded upon divine Scriptures . . . in which Christmas is called Anti-Christ's-masse, and those Masse-mongers and Papists who observe it. . . . In consequence of which, Parliament spent some Time in consultation about the Abolition of Christmas-day, pass'd Orders to that Effect, and resolv'd to sit on the following Day, which was commonly called Christmas-day.

Five years later John Evelyn wrote in his diary as follows:

> I went with my Wife &c: to *Lond*: to celebrate *Christmas day*. Mr. Gunning preaching in *Exesceter* Chapell on 7. *Micha* 2. Sermon Ended, as he was giving us the holy Sacrement, The Chapell was surrounded with Soldiers: All the Communicants and Assembly surpriz'd & kept Prisoners by them, some in the house, others carried away: It fell to my share to be confined to a roome in the house, where yet were permitted to Dine with the master of it, the Countesse of *Dorset*, *Lady Hatton* &c some others of quality who invited me: In the afternoone came *Collonel Whalley*, Goffe & others from *Whitehall* to examine us one by one, & some they committed to the *Martial*, some to Prison, some Committed: When I came before them they tooke my name and aboad, examined me, why contrarie to an Ordinance made that none should any longer observe the superstitious time of the Nativity (so esteem'd by them) I durst offend, & particularly be at *Common prayers*, which they told me was but the *Masse* in *English*, & particularly pray for *Charles* stuard, for which we had no scripture: I told them we did not pray for *Cha*: *Steward* but for all *Christian Kings, Princes and Governors*: They replied, in so doing we praied for the K. of *Spaine* too, who was their enemie, & a *Papist*, with other frivolous & insnaring questions, with much threatning, & finding no colour to detaine me longer, with much pitty of my Ignorance, they dismiss'd me: These men were of high flight, and above Ordinances: & spake spitefull things of our B. Lord nativity: so I got home late the next day blessed be God: These wretched

miscreants, held their muskets against us as we came up to receive the Sacred Elements, as if they would have shot us at the Altar, but yet suffering us to finish the Office of Communion, as perhaps not in their Instructions what they should do in case they found us in that Action.

As a contrast to these sombre annals let us look through a foreigner's eyes at a merrier Christmas as it was celebrated in England just before the turn of the century. The observer is a Frenchman, Henri Misson, who wrote in his *Mémoires d'Angleterre* (1698):

> Le jour de Noël, les Fêtes, & les jours suivans jusqu'aprés les Rois,* est un temps de gayeté Chrêtienne; un melange de Devotion & de Plaisirs. On fait des Voeux les uns pour les autres, on se régale, on cherche tant qu'on peut à banir la Melancholie. Au lieu que les petits présens ne se sont en France que le premier jour de l'An, on commence ici dés Noël. C'est même plutot le jour de Noël que le jour de l'An qu'on les fait: Non pas tant les présens d'Ami à Ami, on d'égal à égal, ce qui ne se pratique plus guére en Angleterre; mais les présens de Superieur à inferieur. Dans les Cabarets, les Hôtes, les Hôtes donnent en partie ce qu'on va boire ou manger chez eux ce jour-là, & les deux Fêtes d'aprés: Ils sont payer le Vin, pour exemple, & disent qu'il n'y a rien pour le pain, ni pour la tranche de Jambon.

Sooner or later, when looking through eye-witness accounts of the past, one comes to that slightly ridiculous but singularly candid self-observer, James Boswell. This is what he wrote in his journal on Christmas Day 1762:

> The night before I did not rest well. I was really violently in love with Louisa. I thought she did not care for me. I thought that if I did not gain her affections, I would appear despicable to myself. This day I was in better frame, being Christmas Day, which always inspired me with most agreeable feelings. I went to St Paul's Church and in that magnificent temple fervently adored the God of goodness and mercy, and heard a sermon by the Bishop of Oxford on the publishing of glad tidings of great joy.

* Aux Rois, on partage le Gateau, & le Roi de la Féve régale la Compagnie.

We move a few years ahead, to Christmas 1790, and away up into Norfolk, where, at Weston Longueville, the Rev. James Woodforde is recording his day:

> *Decem.* 25. Saturday and Christmas Day. I breakfasted, dined, &c. again at home. Nancy breakfasted, dined &c again at home. I read Prayers and administered the H. Sacrament this morning at Weston Church being Christmas Day. Gave for an offering, o.2.6. Mr. and Mrs. Custance at Church and at the Sacrament. Mr. Custance's two eldest Sons were at Church and during the administration of the H. Sacrament were in my Seat in the Chancel to see the whole Ceremony by Mrs. Custance's desire. My old Clerk Js. Smith, old Tom Cary, old Nt. Heavens, old John Peachman, and old Christ. Dunnell dined at my House on rost Beef and Plumb Pudding. I gave also to each to carry home to their Wives 1s od., o.5.o. Sent old Tom Carr not being able to come as being ill, his Dinner, and with it, o.1.o. I lighted my large Wax-Candle being Xmas Day during Tea time this Afternoon for abt. an Hour. It was very mild thank God today for this time of Year tho' wet and very dirty walking. Nancy having herself new made the late Silk Gown I gave her, wore it this Day for the 1st time.

We are looking for eye-witnesses' accounts, but we cannot resist an occasional side-glance at fiction, such as the preparations for Christmas at Headlong Hall, where Thomas Love Peacock's Squire Headlong had invited Mr Foster, the perfectilian, Mr Escot, the deteriorationist, Mr Jenkinson, the status-quo-ite, and the Rev. Doctor Gaster, who had written a learned dissertation on the art of stuffing a turkey, to spend Christmas (circa 1815) with him and take part in the Christmas Ball:

> Squire Headlong, in the mean while, was quadripartite in his locality; that is to say, he was superintending the operations in four scenes of action—namely, the cellar, the library, the picture gallery, and the dining room—preparing for the reception of his philosophical and dilettante visitors. His myrmidon on this occasion was a little red-nosed butler, whom nature seemed to have cast in the genuine mould of an antique Silenus, and who waddled about the house after his master wiping his forehead and panting for breath, while the latter bounced from room to room like a cracker, and was indefatigable in his requisitions for the proximity of

G

his vinous Achates, whose advice and co-operation he deemed no less necessary in the library than in the cellar. Multitudes of packages had arrived, by land and water, from London, and Liverpool, and Chester, and Manchester, and Birmingham, and various parts of the mountains: books, wine, cheese, globes, mathematical instruments, turkeys, telescopes, hams, tongues, microscopes, quadrants, sextants, fiddles, flutes, tea, sugar, electrical machines, figs, spices, air-pumps, soda-water, chemical apparatus, eggs, French-horns, drawing books, palettes, oils and colours, bottled ale and porter, scenery for a private theatre, pickles and fish-sauce, patent lamps and chandeliers, barrels of oysters, sofas, chairs, tables, carpets, beds, looking-glasses, pictures, fruits and confections, nuts, oranges, lemons, packages of salt salmon, and jars of Portugal grapes. These, arriving with infinite rapidity, and inexhaustible succession, had been deposited at random, as the convenience of the moment dictated—sofas in the cellar, chandeliers in the kitchen, hampers of ale in the drawing room, and fiddles and fish sauce in the library. The servants, unpacking all these in furious haste, and flying with them from place to place, according to the tumultuous directions of Squire Headlong and the little fat butler who fumed at his heels, chafed, and crossed, and clashed, and tumbled over one another upstairs and down. All was bustle, uproar and confusion; yet nothing seemed to advance; while the rage and impetuosity of the Squire continued fermenting to the highest degree of exasperation, which he signified from time to time by converting some newly unpacked article, such as a book, a bottle, a ham, or a fiddle, into a missile against the head of some unfortunate servant who did not seem to move in a ratio of velocity corresponding to the intensity of his master's desires.

From Headlong Hall we move on to Bracebridge Hall, which was fictitious in name, but bore a close resemblance to Aston Hall, in Warwickshire. There are obvious parallels between Squire Bracebridge and Sir Roger de Coverley, but there is much to be said for the claim that Washington Irving 'invented' about 1820 what is now popularly known as the 'old-fashioned Christmas'. Here are some passages from *Old Christmas* describing Squire Bracebridge going to church:

As the morning, though frosty, was remarkably fine and clear, the most of the family walked to the church, which was a very old building of gray stone, and stood near a village, about half-a-mile from the park gate. Adjoining it was a low snug parsonage, which seemed coeval with the church. The front of it was perfectly matted with a yew-tree that had been trained against its walls, through the dense foliage of which apertures had been formed to admit light into the small antique lattices. As we passed this sheltered nest, the parson issued forth and preceded us. . . .

On reaching the church-porch, we found the parson rebuking the gray-headed sexton for having used mistletoe among the greens with which the church was decorated. It was, he observed, an un-holy plant, profaned by having been used by the Druids in their mystic ceremonies; and though it might be innocently employed in the festive ornamenting of halls and kitchens, yet it had been deemed by the Fathers of the Church as unhallowed, and totally unfit for sacred purposes. So tenacious was he on this point, that the poor sexton was obliged to strip down a great part of the humble trophies of his taste, before the parson would consent to enter upon the service of the day. . . .

The orchestra was in a small gallery, and presented a most whimsical grouping of heads piled one above the other, among which I particularly noticed that of the village tailor, a pale fellow with a retreating forehead and chin, who played on the clarionet, and seemed to have blown his face to a point; and there was another, a short pursy man, stooping and labouring at a bass viol, so as to show nothing but the top of a round bald head, like the egg of an ostrich. There were two or three pretty faces among the female singers, to which the keen air of a frosty morning had given a bright rosy tint; but the gentlemen choristers had evidently been chosen like old Cremona fiddles, more for tone than looks; and as several had to sing from the same book, there were clusterings of odd physiognomies, not unlike those groups of cherubs we sometimes see on country tombstones.

The usual services of the choir were managed tolerably well, the vocal parts generally lagging a little behind the instrumental, and some loitering fiddler now and then making up for lost time by travelling over a passage with prodigious celerity, and clearing more bars than the keenest foxhunter, to be in at the death. . . .

The parson gave us a most erudite sermon on the rites and ceremonies of Christmas, and the propriety of observing it not merely as a day of thanksgiving, but of rejoicing; supporting the correctness of his opinions by the earliest usages of the Church, and enforcing them by the authorities of Theophilus of Cesarea, St Cyprian, St Chrysostom, St Augustine, and a cloud more of Saints and Fathers, from whom he made copious quotations. . . .

I have seldom known a sermon attended apparently with more immediate effects; for on leaving the church the congregation seemed one and all possessed with the gaiety of spirit so earnestly enjoined by their pastor. The elder folks gathered in knots in the churchyard, greeting and shaking hands; and the children ran about crying, Ule! Ule! and repeating some uncouth rhymes, which the parson, who had joined us, informed me had been handed down from days of yore. The villages doffed their hats to the Squire as he passed, giving him the good wishes of the season with every appearance of heartfelt sincerity, and were invited by him to the hall, to take something to keep out the cold weather; and I heard blessings uttered by several of the poor, which convinced me that, in the midst of his enjoyments, the worthy old cavalier had not forgotten the true Christmas virtue of charity.

Washington Irving, though his father was an Englishman, was born in New York. It is illuminating to compare his impressions of Christmas in rural England with the recollections of a fellow American, Theodore Ledyard Cuyler (1820–1909), of Christmas on a farm in western New York only a year or two later:

As the visits of Santa Claus in the night could only be through the chimney, we hung our stockings where they would be in full sight. Three score and ten years ago such modern contrivances as steam pipes, and those unpoetical holes in the floor called 'hot-air registers', were as entirely unknown in our rural regions as gas-burners or telephones. We had a genuine fire-place in our kitchen, big enough to contain an enormous back-log, and broad enough for eight or ten people to form 'a circle wide' before it and enjoy the genial warmth.

The last process before going to bed was to suspend our stockings in the chimney jambs; and then we dreamed of Santa Claus, or if we awoke in the night, we listened for the jingling of his sleigh-bells. At the peep of day we were aroused by the voice of my good grandfather, who planted himself in the stairway and shouted in a stentorian tone, 'I wish you all a Merry Christmas!' The contest was as to who should give the salutation first, and the old gentleman determined to get the start on us by sounding his greeting to the family before we were out of our rooms. Then came a race for the chimney corner; all the stockings came down quicker than they had gone up. What could not be contained in them was disposed upon the mantlepiece, or elsewhere. I remember that I once received an autograph letter from Santa Claus, full of good counsels; and our coloured cook told me that she awoke in the night and, peeping into the kitchen, actually saw the veritable old visitor light a candle and sit down at the table and write it! I believed it all as implicitly as I believed the Ten Commandments, or the story of David and Goliath. . . .

So far we have seen Christmas almost entirely through the eyes of the rich, or at least the well-to-do. It was not until the early nineteenth century that the voice of the 'under-privileged' was heard, but it is fortunate that one of the first of such voices was that of a singularly gifted poet. In his poetry he has left a vivid and detailed record of the kind of Christmas enjoyed by an English farm labourer and his family just about the same time that Washington Irving was at 'Bracebridge Hall', and Theodore Ledyard Cuyler was a child on that great farm in New York. The verses which follow were written by John Clare at Helpstone, in Northamptonshire, and were published in *The Shepherd's Calendar* in 1827:

> Each house is swept the day before,
>   And windows stuck with evergreens,
> The snow is besom'd from the door,
>   And comfort crowns the cottage scenes.
> Gilt holly, with its thorny pricks
>   And yew and box, with berries small,
> These deck the unused candlesticks,
>   And pictures hanging by the wall . . .
>
> The singing waits, a merry throng,
>   At early morn with simple skill,
> Yet imitate the angel's song,
>   And chant their Christmas ditty still;
> And, mid the storm that dies and swells
>   By fits, in hummings softly steals
> The music of the village bells,
>   Ringing round their merry peals.

When this past, a merry crew,
    Bedeck'd in masks and ribbons gay,
The 'Morris-dance', their sports renew,
    And act their winter evening play.
The clown turn'd king, for penny-praise,
    Storms with the actor's strut and swell;
And Harlequin, a laugh to raise,
    Wears his hunchback and tinkling bell.

And oft for pence and spicy ale,
    With winter nosegays pinn'd before,
The wassail-singer tells her tale,
    And drawls her Christmas carols o'er.
While prentice boy, with ruddy face,
    And rime be-powder'd dancing locks,
From door to door with happy pace,
    Runs round to claim his 'Christmas box'.

It is clear from this poem that Christmas present-giving was an established custom even in the humblest homes in England in the first years of the nineteenth century. That it was also customary in Germany is evident from the journal of George Tickner, an American visiting Dresden in 1835:

In the evening we witnessed some of the results of this very peculiar national feeling and custom; that, I mean, of the children giving presents to the parents and the parents to the children on Christmas Eve. We were invited to witness it at Baron Ungern Sternberg's. At first, in the saloon, we saw the Baron and his wife, whom I had met at Tieck's, people of a good deal of taste and cultivation, and we amused ourselves with looking over some of the drawings and curiosities which the Baron's intimate friend, the Count Stackelberg, brought from Greece, a remarkable collection . . . constituting the materials for the beautiful work which Stackelberg is now publishing. As we were in the midst of looking them over a little bell rang, and we went into the room where the presents which the children had secretly prepared for the elder members of the family were placed under the tree. They were all prepared by two little girls of twelve and fourteen . . . and though there was nothing very valuable or beautiful in what was given, yet it was all received with so much pleasure by the parents and elder brother, that the children were delighted, and kissed us all round very heartily. While this was going on a bell rang in another part of the house, and we were led through a passage-way purposely kept dark, where two folding-doors were thrown open and we were all at once in a large and handsome saloon, which was brilliantly lighted up, and where were the presents which the parents had provided for the children. . . .

Writing of a Christmas in Germany sixty years later, the Countess von Arnim (later the Countess Russell) gave another vivid glimpse of the German Christmas. The book is *Elizabeth and her German Garden* (1898); the scene a castle in Pomerania:

The library is uninhabitable for several days before and after, as it is there that we have the trees and presents. All down one side are the trees, and the other three sides are lined with tables, a separate one for each person in the house. When the trees are lighted, and stand in their radiance shining down on the happy faces, I forget all the trouble it has been, and the number of times I have had to run up and down stairs, and the various aches in head and feet, and enjoy myself as much as anybody. First the June baby is ushered in, then the others and ourselves according to age, then the servants, then come the head inspector and his family, the other inspectors from the different farms, the mamsells, the book-keepers and secretaries, and then all the children, troops and troops of them —the big ones leading the little ones by the hand and carrying the babies in their arms, and the mothers peeping round the door. As many as can get in stand in front of the trees, and sing two or three carols; then they are given their presents, and go off triumphantly, making room for the next batch. My three babies sang lustily too, whether they happened to know what was being sung or not. They had on white dresses in honour of the occasion, and the June baby was even arrayed in a low-necked and short-sleeved garment, after the manner of Teutonic infants, whatever the state of the thermometer. Her arms are like miniature prize-fighter's arms—I never saw such things; they are the pride and joy of her little nurse, who had tied them up with blue ribbons, and kept on kissing them. . . .

When they came to say good-night, they were all very pale and subdued. The April baby had an exhausted-looking Japanese doll with her, which she said she was taking to bed, not because she liked him, but because she was so sorry for him, he seemed so very tired. They kissed me absently, and went away, only the April baby glancing at the trees as she passed, and making them a curtsey.

'Good-bye, trees,' I heard her say; and then she made the Japanese doll bow to them, which he did, in a very languid and blasé fashion. 'You'll never see such trees again,' she told him, giving him a vindictive shake, 'for you'll be brokened long before next time.'

She went out, but came back as though she had forgotten something.

'Thank the *Christkind* so much, Mummy, won't you, for all the lovely things He brought us. I suppose you're writing to Him now, isn't you?'

In France, as we have seen, present-giving was usually deferred until New Year's Eve. That Christmas was nonetheless an important social festivity in the middle of the nineteenth century is apparent from a report by a correspondent in the *Illustrated London News* in 1849:

When Christmas draws near, every family in easy circumstances sends for a cask of wine, and lays in a stock of southern fruits, which, as they arrive, may be seen on the quay in large quantities. In the flower-market, orange branches, with fruit or blossoms, in elegant tubs; as also all kinds of toys for children, and laurel-trees, hung with various kinds of southern fruits; rose-trees in beautiful pots, etc. are set out for sale.

The Christmas evening is devoted to universal joy and festivity; every booth, cellar, coffee-house, Etc. is illuminated, and the table of the poor chestnut-roaster has an additional lamp. The theatres give grand ballets; the gaming houses, balls and *soupers* and the streets are crowded during the whole night with people and bands of music.

That which strangers most admire, and no provincial person ever forgets, even at the greatest distance from his country, is a sort of sacred entertainment, at which the whole family is present.

The relations who have been absent from each other, perhaps during the whole year, are to meet on this evening; those who have been the greatest enemies pardon each other at Christmas; marriages are fixed; married pairs who have been separated are at this time united; the shyest lover becomes eloquent, and the most coy fair one become kind; every heart dilates with good-will, love and tenderness on Christmas evening.

As one goes south, towards the relative warmth and the Latin outlook of the Mediterranean, one might expect to move away from the traditions of Yule-tide which so dominate the Christmas festivities of Northern Europe and North America. Yet we find extraordinary parallels to northern mythology in a land which borders on the Mediterranean. They were described in 1902 by T. A. Janvier in a little book of great charm and interest, *The Christmas Kalends of Provence*:

Presently we were grouped around the devoted almond-tree; a gnarled old personage, of a great age and girth, having that pathetic look of sorrowful dignity which I find always in superannuated trees—and now and then in humans of gentle natures who are conscious that their days of usefulness are gone. Esperit, who was beside me, felt called upon to explain that the old tree was almost past bearing and so was worthless. His explanation seemed to me a bit of needless cruelty; and I was glad when Magali, evidently moved by the same feeling, intervened softly with: 'Hush, the poor tree may understand!' And then added, aloud: 'The old almond must know that it is a very great honour for any tree to be chosen for the Christmas fire! . . .'

Even the children were quiet as old Jan took his place beside the tree, and there was a touch of solemnity in his manner as he swung his heavy axe and gave the first strong blow—that sent a shiver through all the branches, as though the tree realized that death had overtaken it at last. When he had slashed a dozen times into the trunk, making a deep gash in the pale red wood beneath the brown bark, he handed the axe to Marius; and stood watching silently with the rest of us while his son finished the work that he had begun. In a few minutes the tree tottered; and then fell with a growling death-cry, as its brittle old branches crashed upon the ground.

Whatever there had been of unconscious reverence in the

silence that attended the felling was at an end. As the tree came down everybody shouted. Instantly the children were swarming all over it. In a moment our little company burst into the flood of loud and lively talk that is inseparable in Provence from gay occasions—and that is ill held in check even at funerals and in church. . . .

Marius completed his work by cutting through the trunk again, making a noble cacho-fio near five feet long—big enough to burn, according to the Provençal rule, from Christmas Eve until the evening of New Year's Day.

It is not expected, of course, that the log shall burn continuously. Each night it is smothered in ashes and is not set a-blazing again until the following evening. But even when thus husbanded the log must be a big one to last the week out, and it is only in rich households that the rule can be observed. Persons of modest means are satisfied if they can keep burning the sacred fire over Christmas Day; and as to the very poor, their cacho-fio is no more than a bit of a fruit-tree's branch—that barely, by cautious guarding, will burn until the midnight of Christmas Eve. Yet this suffices: and it seems to me that there is something very tenderly touching about these thin yule-twigs which make, with all the loving ceremonial and rejoicing that might go with a whole tree-trunk, the poor man's Christmas fire. . . .

Always the yule-log is brought home in triumph. If it is small, it is carried on the shoulder of the father or the eldest son; if it is a goodly size, those two carry it together; or a young husband and wife may bear it between them—as we actually saw a thick branch of our almond borne away that afternoon—while the children caracole around them or lend little helping hands.

Being come to the Mazet, the log was stood on end in the court-yard in readiness to be taken thence to the fireplace on Christmas Eve. I fancied that the men handled it with a certain reverence; and the Vidame assured me that such actually was the case. Already, being dedicated to the Christmas rite, it had become in a way sacred.

Leaving France, let us illustrate the continuance of French traditions and the French way of feeling in a new land, Canada. The following poem, 'Noël intime: Décembre 1900' is by the Canadian poet, Louis Dantin (1865–1945):

Oh! qu'ils furent heureux, les pâtres de Judée
Eveillés au buccin de l'Ange triomphant,
Et la troupe des Rois par l'étoile guidée
Vers le chaume mystique où s'abritait l'Enfant!

Tous ceux qui, dans la paix de cette nuit agreste,
Trouvèrent le Promis, le Christ enfin venu;
Et ceux même, ignorants de l'Envoyé céleste,
Qui L'avaient repoussé, mais du moins L'avaient vu!

La Mère, s'enivirant d'extase virginale,
Joseph, pour qui tout le mystère enfin à lui,
Et l'étable, et la crèche, et la bise hivernale
Par les vieux ais disjoints se glissant jusqu'à Lui!

Tout ce qui Le toucha dans sa chair ou son âme,
Tout ce que son rayon commença d'éblouir,
Princes savants, bergers pieux, Hérode infâme,
Tout ce qui crut en Lui, fût-ce pour le haïr!

Oh! qu'ils furent heureux. Moi, dans l'ombre muette,
Je m'asseois, pasteur morne et blême de soucis,
Et jamais un archange à ma veille inquiète
Ne vient jeter le *Gloria in Excelsis.*

Je scrute le reflet de toutes les étoiles,
Mage pensif, avec un désir surhumain;
Mais leur front radieux pour moi n'a que des voiles,
Et pas une du doigt ne me montre un chemin.

Et mon âme est la Vierge attendant la promesse,
Mais que ne touche point le souffle de l'Esprit;
Ou le vieillard en pleurs qu'un sombre doute oppresse
Et qui n'a jamais su d'où venait Jésus-Christ.

Je suis l'étable offrant en vain son sol aride
Au Roi toujours lointain et toujours attendu;
Et dans mon cœur voici la crèche, berceau vide,
Où le vent froid gémit comme un espoir perdu.

Thence to South Africa, where Margaret Allonby writes of 'A Book for Christmas':

> From the North the populated breeze
> Brings alive the flying messages.
> Like leaves, red feet relinquish bonny trees.
> In time for Christmas they have booked their passages —
> Over Congo, across the red zone of heat.
> The secret wind they know, in the southern hills,
> Twists about them, curves their course. Their feet
> Clasp last year's rest. How long, how long
> The long month's cry, until our hearts are stirred
> By thrilling news, the birds! We belong
> Who, in these latitudes, with no word,
> No confraternity, no song, cup ear
> To catch the angel sounds, now near and here.

We return to England and a colder clime, though 'Christmas weather', of course, is something of a myth. In England there is seldom snow at Christmas; there is often a period of rather warm, damp weather. Most of the really hard winters have not set in until the middle of January. An exception, however, was the Christmas of 1860, which was thus recorded in the *Illustrated London News* of 29 December:

> In London there has been skating on almost all the park waters, and a fatal accident occurred in the Serpentine on Monday, Mr C. A. Smith, of Halfmoon-street, Piccadilly, being drowned.
>
> Accounts come from all parts of the country of the severity of the temperature. Mr Lowe, the well-known meteorologist, reporting from his observatory at Beeston, 'Perhaps the most extraordinary cold ever known in England—certainly exceeding every record but one, and that record being looked upon as an error, and, indeed, thought to be an impossible temperature in England.'
>
> 'This morning,' he says, writing on Christmas Day, 'the temperature at four feet above the ground was 8 deg. above zero, and on the grass 13.8 deg. below zero, or 45.8 deg. of frost. The Trent is full of ice, and will soon be frozen over. I have just seen a horse pass with icicles at his nose three inches in length and as thick as three fingers.'

Ten years later, as Parson Kilvert recorded in his diary of Christmas 1870, there was severe cold, at least in Clyro, Radnorshire:

Saturday, Christmas Eve. An intense frost in the night. Lowest point 14 degrees. When I went into my bath I sat down amongst a shoal of fragments of broken floating ice as sharp as glass. Everything was frozen stiff and stark, sponge, brushes and all. After I had used the sponge and put it into the basin it was frozen to the basin again in less than 5 minutes. . . .

Sunday, Christmas Day. As I lay awake praying in the early morning I thought I heard a sound of distant bells. It was an intense frost. I sat down in my bath upon a sheet of thick ice which broke in the middle into large pieces whilst sharp points and jagged edges stuck all round the sides of the tub like chevaux de frise, not particularly comforting to the naked thighs and loins, for the keen ice cut like broken glass. The ice water stung and scorched like fire. I had to collect the floating pieces of ice and pile them on a chair before I could use the sponge in my hands for it was a mass of ice. The morning was most brilliant. Walked to the Sunday School with Gibbins and the road sparkled with millions of rainbows, the seven colours gleaming in every glittering point of hoar frost. The Church was very cold in spite of two roaring stove fires.

We have not yet made any mention of a work of literature (if it may so be regarded) which, at any rate in its opening line, is almost as well known throughout the world as 'Good King Wenceslas'. Very few people however, remember more than the opening line, or, if they do, their version is rather different from that which the author, George R. Sims, published in 1903 in a volume entitled *The Dagonet and Other Poems.* In justice to the author of a ballad which has, whatever its limitations, become a classic example of popular art, we venture to reprint some stanzas:

> It is Christmas Day in the Workhouse,
>> And the cold bare walls are bright
> With garlands of green and holly,
>> And the place is a pleasant sight:
> For with clean-washed hands and faces
>> In a long and hungry line
> The paupers sit at the tables
>> For this is the hour they dine.

And the guardians and their ladies,
    Although the wind is east,
Have come in their furs and wrappers,
    To watch their charges feast:
To smile and be condescending,
    Put pudding on pauper plates,
To be hosts at the workhouse banquet
    They've paid for, with the rates.

Oh, the paupers are meek and lowly
    With their 'Thank'ee kindly, mum's'
So long as they fill their stomachs,
    What matter it whence it comes?
But one of the old men mutters
    And pushes his plate aside:
'Great God!' he cries; 'but it chokes me!
    For this is the day *she* died. . . .

'Last winter my wife lay dying,
    Starved in a filthy den;
I'd never been to the parish—
    I came to the parish then.
I swallowed my pride in coming,
    For, ere the ruin came,
I held up my head as a trader,
    And I bore a spotless name.

'I came to the parish, craving
    Bread for my starving wife,
Bread for the woman who'd loved me
    Through fifty years of life;
And what do you think they told me,
    Mocking my awful grief?
That "the House" was open to us,
    But they wouldn't give "out relief".

'I slunk to the filthy alley—
    'Twas a cold, raw Christmas Eve—
And the bakers' shops were open,
    Tempting a man to thieve;

But I clenched my fists together,
    Holding my head away,
So I came to her empty-handed,
    And mournfully told her why.

'Then I told her the "House" was open;
    She had heard of the ways of *that*,
For her bloodless cheeks went crimson,
    And up in her rags she sat,
Crying, "Bide the Christmas here, John,
    We've never had one apart;
I think I can bear the hunger—
    The other would break my heart."

'All through that eve I watched her,
    Holding her hand in mine,
Praying the Lord and weeping
    Till my lips were salt as brine.
I asked her once if she hungered,
    And as she answered "No",
The moon shone in at the window
    Set in a wreath of snow.

'Then the room was bathed in glory,
    And I saw in my darling's eyes,
The far-away look of wonder
    That comes when the spirit flies;
And her lips were parched and parted,
    And her reason came and went,
For she raved of our home in Devon,
    Where our happiest years were spent.

'And the accents long forgotten,
    Came back to the tongue once more,
For she talk'd like the country lassie
    I woo'd by the Devon shore.
Then she rose to her feet and trembled,
    And fell on the rags and moaned,
And, "Give me a crust—I'm famished—
    For the love of God!" she groaned.

'I rushed from the room like a madman
    And flew to the workhouse gate,
Crying "Food for a dying woman!"
    And the answer came, "Too late."
They drove me away with curses;
    Then I fought with a dog in the street,
And tore from the mongrel's clutches,
    A crust he was trying to eat.

'Back, through the filthy by-lanes!
    Back through the trampled slush!
Up to the crazy garret,
    Wrapped in an awful hush.
My heart sank down at the threshold,
    And I paused with a sudden thrill,
For there in the silv'ry moonlight
    My Nance lay, cold and still.

'Up to the blackened ceiling
    The sunken eyes were cast—
I knew on those lips all bloodless
    My name had been the last;
She'd called for her absent husband—
    Oh God! Had I but known!—
Had called in vain, and in anguish
    Had died in that den—*alone*.

'Yes, there, in a land of plenty,
    Lay a loving woman dead,
Cruelly starved and murdered
    For a loaf of the parish bread.
At yonder gate, last Christmas,
    I craved for a human life,
You, who would·feast our paupers,
    What of my murdered wife? . . .

'There, get ye gone to your dinners:
    Don't mind me in the least;
Think of the happy paupers
    Eating your Christmas feast;

And when you recount your blessings
　　In your smug parochial way,
Say what you did for *me*, too,
　　Only last Christmas Day.'

After that strong dose of Victorian sentiment we pass with some relief to the more genial joys of Mr Pooter's Christmas, as recorded in 1891 by his creators, George and Weedon Grossmith, in *The Diary of a Nobody*:

Christmas Day—We caught the 10.20 train at Paddington, and spent a pleasant day at Carrie's mother's. The country was quite nice and pleasant, although the roads were sloppy. We dined in the middle of the day, just ten of us, and talked over old times. If everybody had a nice, *un*interfering mother-in-law, such as I have, what a deal of happiness there would be in the world. Being all in good spirits, I proposed her health, and I made, I think, a very good speech.

I concluded, rather neatly, by saying: 'On such an occasion as this—whether relatives, friends or acquaintances—we are all inspired with good feelings towards each other. Those who have quarrelled with absent friends should kiss and make it up. Those who happily have *not* fallen out, can kiss all the same.'

I saw tears in the eyes of both Carrie and her mother, and must say I felt very flattered by the compliment. That dear old Reverend John Panzy Smith, who married us, made a most cheerful and amusing speech, and said he should act on my suggestion respecting the kissing. He then walked round the table and kissed all the ladies, including Carrie. Of course one did not object to this; but I was more than staggered when a young fellow named Moss, who was a stranger to me, and who had scarcely spoken a word through dinner, jumped up suddenly with a sprig of mistletoe, and ex-claimed: 'Hulloh! I don't see why I shouldn't be in on this scene.' Before one could realise what he was about to do, he kissed Carrie and the rest of the ladies. Fortunately the matter was treated as a joke, and we all laughed; but it was a dangerous experiment, and I felt very uneasy for a moment as to the result. I subsequently referred to the matter to Carrie, but she said, 'Oh, he's not much more than a boy.' I said that he had a very large moustache for a boy. Carrie replied: 'I didn't say he was not a nice boy.'

H

Our candles of reminiscence have now lighted our steps into our own time—into an era when most of us are able to look back upon memories of our own. We can none of us share, however, the sensations of Captain Scott on Christmas Day 1910. During the course of that last journey, from which he never returned, he wrote to his wife:

> I looked out-of-doors in the evening on a truly Christmassy scene. On all sides an expanse of snow-covered floes, a dull grey sky shedding fleecy snow flakes, every rope and spar had its little white deposit like the sugaring on a cake. A group of penguins were having highly amusing antics close by, and the sounds of revelry followed behind, but on the white curtain of feathery crystals I tried to picture your face, and I said God bless her for having been an unselfish wife, and the best of friends to an undeserving man.

And very few of us, we imagine, can recollect at first hand what was perhaps the most dramatic and moving expression of the Christmas spirit in modern times—the suspension of hostilities on the Western Front during the first Christmas of the First World War. Here are the words of an anonymous eye-witness, as broadcast many years later:

> Nobody can tell you the whole true story of that incredible Christmas truce of the First World War. . . . The Germans unquestionably began it—almost certainly the Saxons. . . . Men of the North Staffordshire Regiment found themselves exchanging 'words of good cheer' with their opposite numbers. Then they got up and sat on the parapet, talking across No Man's Land to each other. A British officer suggested a *Volkslied*. The Germans agreed eagerly, both sides singing in turn. . . . A truce was agreed upon until midnight on Christmas Day. It took the shape at first of both sides helping one another to bury their dead.
> In another part of the line the troops walked about arm in arm, photographing each other, while the Germans facing a Highland Regiment began by a cornet player rendering 'Home Sweet Home' perfectly, followed by a hymn tune. They then got out of their trenches and walking smilingly towards the Scots. When an officer tried to stop them they said rather pathetically—'But this is Christmas—aren't you Scotsmen Christians too?'
> It ended half diffidently—a gradual return to the normality of killing each other—with both sides firing warning shots in the air.

CHRISTMAS IN WARTIME

The antithesis of peace and war, hatred and goodwill, Mars and Saturn, Christmas and Armageddon, has in our own time given an undercurrent of agony to many Christmas poems. Here is a young American poet, Robert Lowell, writing in the Second World War of his impressions as he stands on Christmas Eve under the statue of Joe Hooker, the great American soldier of the last century:

> Tonight a blackout. Twenty years ago
> I hung my stocking on the tree, and hell's
> Serpent entwined the apple in the toe
> To sting the child with knowledge. Hooker's heels
> Kicking at nothing in the shifting snow,
> A cannon and a cairn of cannon balls
> Rusting before the blackened Statehouse, know
> How the long horn of plenty broke like glass
> In Hooker's gauntlets. Once I came from Mass;
>
> Now storm-clouds shelter Christmas, once again
> Mars meets his fruitless star with open arms,
> His heavy saber flashes with the rime,
> The war-god's bronzed and empty forehead forms
> Anonymous machinery from raw men;
> The cannon on the Common cannot stun
> The blundering butcher as he rides on Time—
> The barrel clinks with holly. I am cold:
> I asked for bread, my father gives me mould;
>
> His stocking is full of stones. Santa in red
> Is crowned with wizened berries. Man of war,
> Where is the summer's garden? In its bed
> The ancient speckled serpent will appear,
> And black-eyed susan with her frizzled head.
> When Chancellorsville mowed down the volunteer,
> 'All wars are boyish', Herman Melville said;
> But we are old, our fields are running wild:
> Till Christ again turn wanderer and child.

Sombre though the occasion may have been, we observe that Robert Lowell's first impulse on Christmas Eve was to return to his childhood. And, since the birth of a child was the first occasion of it all, we will end this glance through the pages of the album with another memory of childhood: Dylan Thomas, looking back to his childhood in Wales:

I would go out, school-capped and gloved and mufflered, with my bright new boots squeaking, into the white world on to the seaward hill, to call on Jim and Dan and Jack and to walk with them through the silent snowscape of our town.

We went padding through the streets, leaving huge deep footprints in the snow, on the hidden pavements.

'I bet people'll think there's been hippoes.'

'What would you do if you saw a hippo coming down Terrace Road?'

'I'd go like this, bang! I'd throw him over the railings and roll him down the hill and then I'd tickle him under the ear and he'd wag his tail. . . .'

'What would you do if you saw *two* hippoes?. . .'

Iron-flanked and bellowing he-hippoes clanked and blundered and battered through the scudding snow towards us as we passed Mr Daniel's house.

'Let's post Mr Daniel a snowball through his letter-box.'

'Let's write things in the snow.'

'Let's write "Mr Daniel looks like a spaniel" all over his lawn.'

'Look,' Jack said, 'I'm eating snow pie.'

'What's it taste like?'

'Like snow-pie,' Jack said.

Or we walked on the white shore.

'Can the fishes see it's snowing?'

'They think it's the sky falling down.'

The silent one-clouded heavens drifted on to the sea.

'All the old dogs have gone.'

Dogs of a hundred mingled makes yapped in the summer at the sea-rim and yelped at the trespassing mountains of the waves.

'I bet St Bernards would like it now.'

And we were snowblind travellers lost in the north hills, and the great dewlapped dogs, with brandy-flasks round their necks, ambled and shambled up to us, baying 'Excelsior'.

We returned home through the desolate poor sea-facing streets where only a few children fumbled with bare red fingers in the thick wheel-rutted snow and cat-called after us, their voices fading away, as we trudged uphill, into the cries of the dock-birds and the hooters of ships out in the white and whirling bay.

Paper Decorations. Photograph by Edwin Smith.

Francis Wheatley, R.A. (1747–1801). The Mistletoe Bough. *Messrs. M. Bernard.*

10

Boxing Day

The name Boxing Day is not very old. Johnson in his *Dictionary* defined Christmas-box as 'a little box in which little presents are collected at Christmas'. He substantiated this by quoting from Gay's *Trivia* of 1716:

> When time comes round, a Christmas-box they bear,
> And one day makes them rich for all the year.

The incongruity of Christmas observances is illustrated by the fact that this agreeable but trivial practice should have quite submerged the implications of the Feast Day of the first Christian martyr, St Stephen, a day whose original description in the Acts of the Apostles is one of the noblest and most tragic passages in the Bible.

Surprisingly, and quite incongruously, this fearless, eloquent, and noble man has become the patron saint of horses: a fact once acknowledged in Britain—where that animal still retains a little of the air of a deity—but now, we imagine, almost entirely forgotten. As a preacher Stephen became a great missionary, and legend has it that he was one of the first to visit Sweden (where this story is recorded). He had five horses—two red, two white, and one dappled. As soon as one wearied, Stephen mounted another, and, as it were by means of post horses, was able to travel great distances and preach to innumerable concourses. Unhappily, he was travelling through a dark forest when heathens set upon and murdered him. They tied his body on to an unbroken colt, which set off and of its own accord carried the corpse without a stop to Stephen's home at Norrtalje. There his grave became the place of pilgrimage to which sick horses were brought for healing.

There are, or perhaps were, sacred horse rituals in northern Europe: the decking of horses, racing, the blessing of horses, and ceremonial and special feeding of them on St Stephen's day. In England they were bled at the feast, for this was said to benefit them. It seems that these customs were pagan survivals which in due course attached themselves to the saint on whose day they were performed.

There is yet another legend about St Stephen: that he was, at the time of the Nativity, a servant of King Herod. He was vouchsafed a sight of the star over Bethlehem and forsook his liege for the service of the Child.

However, the name of Stephen only survives today in popular Christmas lore because King Wenceslas looked out 'on the Feast of Stephen'. The Martyr's Day has become the mundane Boxing Day. William Sandys did his best to seek a higher sanction for Boxing Day than the importunities of servants and apprentices:

> Some have derived the Christmas box from the practice of the monks to offer masses for the safety of all vessels that went long voyages, in each of which a box, under the control of the priest, was kept for offerings; this was opened at Christmas, whence the name arose: but this does not seem a probable derivation. Apprentices, journeymen, and servants even of the higher classes, such as butlers of the Inns of Court, had these boxes. John Taylor (1580–1654), the 'water poet', without due reverence to the law, compared Westminster Hall to a butler's box, at Christmas, among gamesters; for whosoever loseth the box will be sure to be a winner. Some of these were earthen boxes, with a slit to receive money, and were broken after the collection was made; similar boxes of wood may still be seen. Many entries may be found in old accounts in the nature of Christmas boxes, and the kings of France indeed used to give presents to their soldiers at this time.

Pottery money boxes are well known. Old specimens in various forms, sometimes clearly designed for special purposes, still exist. Yet rather strangely it seems that none can be connected with Christmas practice.

The custom of annually giving presents to paid servants or those that render some regular service is quite distinct from the custom of giving presents to one's friends, and is very old. In countries that observe Christmas enthusiastically it is usual to do so at that feast. Where New Year's Day is the great day of celebration, as in France, then that is the occasion of the usually enforced presentation of the *étrennes*. So long ago as 1419 a regulation was made that the Serjeants and other officers of the Mayor, Sheriffs or City (of London) should not beg for Christmas gifts. Doubtless it was not the first, and certainly it was not the last, of many similar and equally futile attempts to end the custom.

Innumerable account-books of the past record these payments. The accounts of James Brydges, Duke of Chandos, builder of the extravagant mansion of Canons near Edgware, may be taken as showing the distri-

bution of 'boxes' on a ducal scale. In 1737 the waifs got ten shillings. Five shillings each went to the wig-maker's servant, the train-band, the beadle, and the foreign newsman. At half-a-crown a head were the Drury Lane, Haymarket, and Lincoln's Inn playbill men, the three postmen, the watchman. The chimney sweep had no more than a shilling. On a much higher level—a guinea each—were the opera-box keeper, the King's footman, the Yeoman of the Guard, and a special messenger named Jacob Wall.

On a smaller, more personal scale, many of the diarists, such as Samuel Pepys, mention giving money at Christmas. Dean Swift in 1711 recorded in his *Journal to Stella*:

I gave Patrick half-a-crown for his Christmas-box, on condition he would be good, and he came home drunk at midnight. I have taken a memorandum of it; because I never design to give him a groat more.

Besides those who had some substantial grounds for the request, carol singers, mummers, and other itinerant Christmas performers—and the beggar in the rhyme—all claimed a contribution to the 'box' for a virtually non-existent service.

Another observance of St Stephen's Day is concerned, not with the importunities of mankind, but with a strange vendetta against one of

The Wren. Wood engraving by Thomas Bewick

the smallest—and most endearing—of birds, the wren. The ceremony of Hunting the Wren usually, though not in every locality where it occurred, was carried out on St Stephen's Day. One rhyme that belongs to the ceremony says:

> The wren, the wren, the king of all birds
> On St Stephen's day was caught in the furze.

A legend has it that St Stephen was about to escape when a wren sang its noisy song and awakened his guards.

The Hunting of the Wren is one of the numerous reversal ceremonies so typical of Christmastide. Throughout the year the wren is undisputed king of the birds. He gained this honour, a little deceitfully, by nestling unseen on the back of an eagle, and when that great bird had flown as high as he could, jumping off and flying still a little higher. Generally, it is considered unlucky to harm the wren. But on one day in the year he is pursued ruthlessly to death.

In Ireland the custom lingers on as no more than a form of begging. Children in old clothes, their faces blackened, wander about singing a few doggerel lines connected with the hunt, and call on householders for money. In other places the body of a wren is paraded about ritually in a furze-bush. In Cornwall and Oxfordshire the carriers of the tiny corpse pretend that it is of immense weight. In the Isle of Man it was hoisted on a pole; in Wales it was borne in a decorated wren-house.

The custom is unknown in Scotland, but in France was a much more complex ritual—the killer of the first wren became the king.

The learned E. A. Armstrong tells us that the cult reached Britain during the Bronze Age, when cultural inspiration flowed here from the Mediterranean. It was a solar magico-cultural belief, a ceremonial having as its purpose the defeat of the dark earth-powers and identification with the hoped-for triumph of light and life.

Has this custom some remote link with two sporting occasions now well established on Boxing Day? The Boxing Day meet of foxhounds, when children and a particularly large number of visitors are present, is now something of a social and sporting ritual. So is the Boxing Day shoot—on which occasion the afternoon aim of the guns is liable to certain imperfections, but the lunch is usually of peculiar excellence.

The heartier recreations of Boxing Day are sketched by George Huddesford in *Salmagundi* (1791). He invokes Christmas, 'Patron of the festive hearth':

> Who, tho' the Winter chill the skies,
> Canst catch the glow of exercise,
> Following swift the foot-ball's course;
> Or with unresisted force,
> Where Frost arrests the harden'd tide,
> Shooting 'cross the rapid slide.
> Who, e'er the misty morn is grey
> To some high covert hark'st away;

While Sport, on lofty courser borne,
In concert winds his echoing horn
With the deeply-thund'ring hounds,
Whose clangour wild, and joyful sounds,
While Echo swells the doubling cry,
Shake the woods with harmony . . .
Or, if the blast of Winter keen
Spangles o'er the silvery green,
Booted high thou lov'st to tread
Marking, thro' the sedgy mead,
Where the creeping moor-hen lies
Or snipes with sudden twitt'ring rise.
Or joy'st the early walk to take
Where, thro' the pheasant-haunted brake
Oft as the well-aim'd gun resounds,
The eager-dashing spaniel bounds.

From the earliest times to the present day, from the medieval Latin liturgical plays to *Aladdin and his Wonderful Lamp on Ice*, Christmastide —and usually Boxing Day in particular—has been associated with dramatic and spectacular scenes and displays.

On the early history of this Christmas drama a heavy weight of scholarship now lies. In spite of this, and the disadvantage that the language is now largely incomprehensible to us, the medieval miracle plays—many of which apply to the Nativity and its related happenings —are from time to time brought to life, usually on a stage, or in part of a church, perhaps embellished with tasteful dresses and music, and effectively revived in circumstances as extremely remote as possible from their original presentations. When originally performed, by the laity of the Church, or the Guilds, or by the common people as remnants of pagan folk plays in the vital yet gullible atmosphere of medieval times, the highest spirituality rubbed shoulders with the crudest, earthiest fun.

Remains exist of early Latin plays, and of later medieval Christmas plays in the tongues of Germany, France, Spain, and England. We are authoritatively told that the English were surpassed by no foreigners in their treatment of Christmas subjects. Among others we have early versions of the texts of the York Nativity Play, the plays concerning Herod, the Magi, and the Slaughter of the Innocents presented by the Shearmen and Tailors of Coventry, and the Chester and the Towneley plays, with their racy shepherds. With the rise of Protestantism these plays gradually lost their richness, and soon after the Reformation they virtually disappeared. The happy mingling of the shepherds Coll, Gib, and Daw, the thief Mak, Joseph, Mary, Angels, Herod, Jasper, Balthasar, and Melchior, came to an end.

The folk-players continued the pagan tradition, and in Court circles masques became a part of the celebration of the Twelve Days. Edward Hall described their coming to the Court of Henry VIII in 1512:

Against New Yeeres night was made in the hall a castell, gates, towers and dungeon, garnished with artillerie and weapon, after the most warlike fashion: and on the front of the castell was written *Le fortresse dangereux*, and, within the castell were six ladies clothed in russet satin, laid all over with leaves of gold, and everie one knit with laces of blew silke and gold. On their heads, coifs and caps all of gold. After this castell had been carried about the hall, and the queene had beheld it, in came the king with five other, apparelled in coats, the one halfe of russet sattin, the other halfe of rich cloth of gold; on their heads caps of russet sattin embrodered with works of fine gold bullion.

These six assaulted the castell. The ladies seeing them so lustie and couragious, were content to solace with them, and upon further communication to yeeld the castell, and so they came downe and dansed a long space. And after, the ladies led the knights into the castell, and then the castell suddenly vanished out of their sights. On the daie of the Epiphanie at night, the king, with eleven other, were disguised, after the manner of Italie; called a maske, a thing not seene before, in England; they were aparalled in garments long and broad, wrought all with gold, with visors and caps of gold. And, after the banket done, these maskers came in, with six gentlemen disguised in silke, bearing staffe torches, and desired the ladies to danse; some were content and some refused. And, after they had dansed, and communed together, as the fashion of the maske is, they took their leave and departed, and so did the queene and all the ladies.

The masque continued to be in favour for Court celebrations, and in the days of Inigo Jones the mechanics of its staging and scenery reached marvellous heights of ingenuity and beauty.

Few of the masques performed during the Twelve Days had any particular connexion with the season. There was, for example, Thomas Campion's *Masque, Presented in the Banqueting roome at Whitehall, on St Stephen's night last: At the mariage of the right Honourable the Earle of Somerset, & the right noble the Lady Frances Howard*. That was in 1603. It had no connexion whatever with St Stephen; Campion wrote: 'I grounded my whole Inuention upon Inchantmens and several transformations: The work-manship wherof was vndertaken by *M. Constantine*, an Italian, Architect to our late Prince *Henry* . . .'

Ben Jonson, however, was entirely seasonable with *The Masque of Christmas* in 1616. In it we see many of the traditional figures, including Christmas himself, who enters before the Court, 'with two or three of the Guard, attired in round Hose, long Stockings, a close Doublet, a high-crowned Hat, with a Brooch, a long thin Beard, a Truncheon, little Ruffes, white Shoos, his Scarfes and Garters tied cross, and his Drum beaten before him'—a very different figure from our Santa Claus.

Here are all the members and customs of the old Christmastide duly assembled. Included are the mummers or guisers, whose plays and traditions are also the subject of a considerable literature.

By the eighteenth century the masques had disappeared, owing to the rapid development of the theatre, which had taken on pantomimes as the 'traditional Christmas entertainments of the British theatre'. These originated with the comic dances of the Arlequins of the Paris fairs; early in the century they had become an extraordinary mixture of classical tales, harlequinades, and elaborate scenery no doubt inherited from the masques: a 'succession of monstrous medlies'. In the seventeen-twenties John Rich, manager of the theatre at Lincoln's Inn Fields and later of the Theatre Royal, Covent Garden, and Colley Cibber and his joint manager Booth, of Drury Lane, tried to rival one another with extravagant mimed plays in which Harlequin was combined with the legend of Dr Faustus. To them the crowds flocked;

George Cruikshank (1792–1878). A Christmas Box. Coloured etching. 1826. *British Museum.*

Toy Theatre by Pollock, with pantomime in progress. Photograph by
Edwin Smith.

they were 'frequented by persons of the first quality in England to the twentieth and thirtieth time'. In 1728 Alexander Pope gave a description of these and other pantomimes in which:

> All sudden, gorgons hiss, and dragons glare
> And ten-horn'd fiends and giants rush to war.
> Hell rises, Heaven descends, and dance on earth
> Gods, imps and monsters, music, rage and mirth,
> A fire, a jig, a battle and a ball,
> Till one wide conflagration swallows all.
> Thence a new world to Nature's laws unknown,
> Breaks out refulgent, with a heaven its own:
> Another Cynthia* her new journey runs,
> And other planets circle other suns.
> The forests dance, the rivers upward rise,
> Whales sport in woods, and dolphins in the skies;
> And last, to give the whole creation grace,
> Lo! one vast egg produces human race . . .†

> Immortal Rich! how calm he sits at ease
> 'Mid snows of paper, and fierce hail of pease;
> And proud his mistress' orders to perform,
> Rides in the whirlwind and directs the storm.
> But lo! to dark encounter in mid air
> New Wizards rise; I see my Cibber there!
> Booth in his cloudy tabernacle shrin'd,
> On grinning dragons thou shalt mount the wind.
> Dire is the conflict, dismal is the din,
> Here shouts all Drury, there all Lincoln's Inn;
> Contending theatres our empire raise,
> Alike their labours, and alike their praise.

Throughout the eighteenth century the theatres continued to contend in novelty and variety to attract the Christmas audiences. The general form the pantomime took was a fantastically dramatized and versified variation of some well-known tale, the dénouement being a transformation scene. This was followed by the broad comedy of

* The moon.

† In one pantomime, Harlequin was hatched out of an egg.

clown and pantaloon and the dancing of Columbine and Harlequin.

At the beginning of the nineteenth century there appeared the greatest of all pantomimists, Joseph Grimaldi (1779–1837). Grimaldi came of a family of dancers and clowns; it was as a dancer that he first appeared, when he was still an infant. In 1781 he first worked in pantomime, and he was long associated with Drury Lane. He was a man of unusual hobbies—pigeon breeding and entomology; he collected four thousand specimens of flies. Charles Dickens edited his memoirs.

Pantomime spread, and in the middle of the nineteenth century it was at its most popular. The names both of the theatres and the pantomimes that opened on Boxing Night 1850 are so romantic that merely to list them is to share in the pleasure they must have provided:

Lyceum: *King Charming; or the Blue Bird of Paradise*
Sadler's Wells: *Harlequin and the House that Jack Built in 1851* (an allusion to the Great Exhibition)
Haymarket: *The Second Calendar and the Queen of Beauty*
Princess: *Alonzo the Brave and the Fair Imogen*
Olympic: *Princess Dorus or the Romance of the Nose*
Drury Lane: *Harlequin and Humpty Dumpty, or Big Bellied Ben and the First Lord Mayor of London*

The 'transpontine theatre, the Surrey', wrote a critic, 'has turned *The Merry Wives of Windsor* into a harlequinade . . . it may, perhaps, be permitted to pass without censure'. At the Adelphi:

Mr Albert Smith presents us with *The Tarantula or the Spider King*. The piece opens with a scene representing the Realm of Reptiles, in which *Spiderion*, the King of the Spiders, and other unearthly objects, are brought into notice so as to constitute a Monster Meeting, which is terminated in a skilful manner by its transformation into a cloud. In a subsequent scene the height of the ridiculous is attained in a 'coaching scene', in which a car is introduced, drawn by horses made of boys, two to each horse.

Luigi (Miss Woolgar) is the victim of the tarantula, receiving what is supposed to be a fatal bite; and, on the strength of this, *Luigi's* betrothed, *Loretta* (Madame Celeste), is affianced to *Dr Omeopatico* (Mr Wright) but *Luigi's* recovery slightly damages the secondary arrangement, and restores the *status quo*. In the course of the piece 'the village in flames' furnishes opportunity for a very brilliant and effective scene.

So wrote a gentleman dispatched to report on it for *The Illustrated London News* of 28 December 1850. We note that the part of Luigi was played by an actress. The convention of a girl taking the hero's part—the Principal Boy—was started in 1820.

Even Astley's, the home of the circus, joined all the other theatres in putting on 'a pantomime, or extravaganza, for the special gratification of the Christmas visitor'. It was an 'equestrian drama, an altogether grand affair: *Harlequin and Donoghue; or the White Horse of Killarney* is unrivalled for gorgeousness of effect. It was preceded by the spectacle of Kenilworth, thus filling for an entire evening the eye with magnificence.'

The laureate of the pantomime at this period was William Makepeace Thackeray. In his *Sketches and Travels in London* he epitomized and caricatured a visit to the pantomime with great personal enjoyment:

The composer of the Overture of the New Grand Comic Christmas Pantomime, *Harlequin and the Fairy of the Spangled Pocket-handkerchief, or the Prince of the Enchanted Nose*, arrayed in a bran-new Christmas suit, with his wristbands and collar turned elegantly over his cuffs and embroidered satin tie, takes a place at his desk, waves his stick and away the Pantomime Overture begins.

I pity a man who can't appreciate a Pantomime Overture. Children do not like it: they say, 'Hang it, I wish the Pantomime would begin'; but for us it is always a pleasant moment of reflection and enjoyment. It is not difficult music to understand. . . . But of the proper Pantomime-music I am a delighted connoisseur. Perhaps it is because you meet so many old friends in these compositions consorting together in the queerest manner, and occasioning numberless pleasant surprises. Hark! there goes 'Old Dan Tucker' wandering into 'The Groves of Blarney'; our friends the 'Scots wha hae wi' Wallace bled' march rapidly down 'Wapping Old Stairs', from which the '*Figlia del Reggimento*' comes bounding briskly, when she is met, embraced, and carried off by 'Billy Taylor', that brisk young fellow.

All this while you are thinking with a faint, sickly kind of hope, that perhaps the Pantomime *may* be a good one; something like Harlequin and the Golden Orange Tree, which you recollect in your youth. . . . Lives there the man with soul so dead, the being ever so blasé and travel-worn, who does not feel some shock and thrill still: just at that moment when the bell (the dear and familiar bell of your youth) begins to tingle, and the curtain to rise, and the large shoes and ankles, the flesh-coloured leggings, the crumpled knees, the gorgeous robes and masks finally, of the actors ranged on the stage to shout the opening chorus?

All round the house you hear a great gasping a-ha-a from a thousand children's throats. Enjoyment is going to give place to Hope. Desire is about to be realized. O you blind little brats! Clap your hands, and crane over the boxes, and open your eyes with happy wonder! Clap your hands now. In three weeks more the Reverend Doctor Swishtail expects the return of his young friends to Sugarcane House.

But not everyone was pleased. John Ruskin disapproved of panto-mime in a rather different way from Pope. In one of those *Twenty-five Letters to a Working Man of Sunderland on the Laws of Work*, written on 25 February 1867, called 'The Corruption of Modern Pleasure—Covent Garden Pantomime', Ruskin wrote, after a considerable and lofty-minded preamble:

The Pantomime was, as I said, *Ali Baba and the Forty Thieves*. The forty thieves were girls. The forty thieves had forty companions, who were girls. The forty thieves and their forty companions were in some way mixed up with about four hundred and forty fairies, who were girls. There was an Oxford and Cambridge boat-race, in which the Oxford and Cambridge men were girls. There was a transformation scene, with a forest, in which the flowers were girls, and a chandelier, in which the lamps were girls, and a great rainbow which was all of girls.

Mingled incongruously with these seraphic, and, as far as my boyish experience extends, novel, elements of pantomime, there were yet some of its old and fast-expiring elements. There were, in speciality, two thoroughly good pantomime actors—Mr W. H. Payne and Mr Frederick Payne. All that these two did, was done admirably. There were two subordinate actors, who played, subordinately well, the fore and hind legs of a donkey. And there

John Brandard (1812–63). Lithograph for the music score for *Cinderella* pantomime, c. 1860.

'The Merry Christmas Polka'. Engraved music title by T. H. Jones, c. 1870.

was a little actress of whom I have chiefly to speak, who played exquisitely the little part she had to play. The scene in which she appeared was the only one in the whole pantomime in which there was any dramatic effect, or, with a few rare exceptions, any dramatic possibility. It was the home scene, in which Ali Baba's wife, on washing day, is called upon by butcher, baker and milkman, with unpaid bills; and in the extremity of her distress hears her husband's knock at the door, and opens it for him to drive in his donkey, laden with gold. The children who have been beaten instead of getting breakfast, presently share in the raptures of their father and mother; and the little lady I spoke of—eight or nine years old— dances a *pas-de-deux* with the donkey.

She did it beautifully and simply, as a child ought to dance. She was not an infant prodigy; there was no evidence, in the finish or strength of her motion, that she had been put to continual torture through half her eight or nine years. She did nothing more than any child, well taught, but painlessly, might easily do. She caricatured no older person—attempted no curious or fantastic skill. She was dressed decently—she looked and behaved in-nocently—and she danced her joyful dance with perfect grace, spirit, sweetness and self-forgetfulness. And through all the vast theatre, full of English fathers and mothers and children, there was not one hand lifted to give her sign of praise but mine.

Presently after this, came on the forty thieves, who, as I told you, were girls; and, there being no thieving to be presently done, and time hanging heavy on their hands, arms, and legs, the forty thief-girls proceeded to light forty cigars. Whereupon the British public gave them a round of applause. Whereupon I fell a thinking; and saw little more of the piece, except as an ugly and disturbing dream.

A great change in the style of pantomime was brought about by Augustus Harris when he took over Drury Lane in the eighteen-eighties. For long the Principal Boy, in varying forms, and, particularly since Grimaldi, the clown, had been outstanding characters. Now the clown became eclipsed as the comedian by the Dame, and eventually the clown retired to the circus. And it was a Dame recruited from the music-hall who first brought this part of a man burlesquing a woman to the top of the bill. Dan Leno was born within a few days of Christmas in

1860. Coming of theatrical stock, he first appeared on the stage aged four as 'Little George, the Infant Wonder, Contortionist and Posturer'. Soon after making a success on the music-hall stage he was engaged for Drury Lane pantomime as the Dame in 1888. He was a small, slight man with 'a wizened marmosettish face, and in repose melancholy'. For the rest of his life he appeared in every Drury Lane pantomime.

As the twentieth century progressed, pantomime became more and more stereotyped in its form. The titles became restricted to a dozen or so well-known nursery rhymes or fairy stories: *Little Miss Muffet*, *Cinderella*, *Aladdin*, and so on. Actors and actresses from the music-halls took the principal parts: Clarice Mayne, Ella Retford, Tom Foy, Harry Tate, Billy Merson, and the great George Robey—often bringing with them one of their acts from the 'halls'. Gradually, London tired of it. Devotedly the provinces held on, and in the strongholds provincial pantomime played nearly until Easter. But, alas, it is not now faring so well.

The circus, today, is Christmas holiday fare, but not pre-eminently so, since the majority of circuses are peregrinatory affairs, and as much of the history of this ancient entertainment belongs to the rural fairground as to the sawdust rings of Olympia or Madison Square Gardens.

A unique entertainment that is especially associated with Boxing Day is Sir James Barrie's *Peter Pan*. This was first produced on 27 December 1904 at the Duke of York's Theatre, London. It has been revived at Christmas very many times since. Barrie never doubted that it would succeed, though a number of people, then as now, thought it a very odd entertainment. But has it not all the elements of popular—even folk—entertainment? The boy hero—played by a woman (the first to do so was Nina Boucicault); the semi-human animal, the dog-nurse Nana; the good Red Indians; the bad but comic pirates, with Smee and Starkey, and Captain Hook at their head; a house in the tree-tops (something deeply atavistic, this)—and fairies that really fly. This last is a typical pantomime feature. No wonder that Boxing Day, for many, many celebrants under the age of ten, means not St Stephen, but Wendy and Peter.

11

From the Second Day to the Fifth

John, the Apostle and Evangelist, son of Zebedee the fisherman of Galilee, and Salome, and brother of James, was 'the disciple whom Jesus loved'. St John's Day is 27 December, the Second Day of Christmas. Attached to it is a pagan custom that cannot be directly connected with his person; it concerns the blessing (and consumption) of wine, and is carried out in Catholic Germany and Austria. At a ceremony called the *Johannissegen* wine is blessed by the priest. St John's wine has many attributes, according to locality. It keeps other wine standing near it good, and its possessor will have a good harvest; it prevents the drinker from being struck by lightning, is useful as a medicine, and is health-giving. On St John's Day babes join in drinking it. It is hardly surprising that there is also a heavy consumption of ordinary wine, quite apart from that which is blessed.

A similar custom was formerly practised on St Stephen's Day—confirming its irrelevance to St John; presumably it is a relic of an ancient wine sacrifice.

Another extraordinary ceremony is the walk taken on this day by the Masonic Lodge of St John at Melrose in Roxburghshire. In 1707, for no apparent reason, they decided to take a walk in a company with the Grand Master, wearing clean aprons and gloves. The brethren assemble at the George and Abbotsford Hotel, where they collect lighted torches. Then, led by a silver band, they proceed to the Abbey where a short service is held. They then return by torchlight. In the walk the Mercat Cross is encircled three times, and the burial spot of King Robert the Bruce once.

John Evelyn, when in Rome in 1644, made a note that on this day 'A great Supper is given the poore at the Hosp: of s: Jo: Laterano'.

The following day, the Third, commemorates the Childermas, the massacre of the Innocents:

> Herod, when he saw that he was mocked of the wise men, was exceeding wroth; and sent forth, and slew all the children that were in Bethlehem, and in all the coasts thereof, from two years old and under, according to the time which he had diligently enquired of the wise men. Then was fulfilled that which was spoken by Jeremy the prophet, saying, In Rama was there a voice heard, lamentation, and weeping, and great mourning, Rachel weeping for her children, and would not be comforted, because they are not.

Herod, according to some early writers, was a man of great barbarity who committed crimes so terrible that the slaughter of a few Jewish children was insignificant among them. But this appalling reputation cannot be proved. What he ordered at Bethlehem is sufficient to have blackened his name in perpetuity.

The celebration honouring the children who were slaughtered does not, of course, coincide with the massacre itself in accordance with our chronology of the Twelve Days. It was not until after the last of them, Epiphany, that Herod realized he had been deceived by the Magi, and murdered the infants. In the meantime, the Angel of the Lord had appeared to Joseph in a dream, saying: 'Arise, and take the young child, and his mother, and flee into Egypt, and be thou there until I bring thee word; for Herod will seek the young child to destroy him.' And so the family departed into Egypt.

Childermas is an old word, in use at least before the year 1,000. The Feast of the Innocents has been kept by the Church since the fifth century, and the children are regarded as martyrs, though not treated liturgically as such. According to some authorities, the explanation why the Third Day of Christmas was chosen for its celebration was because it commemorates the birth, not the slaughter, of the victims.

A tradition firmly attached to this day has now, it seems, quite disappeared. It was considered one of the unluckiest days in the year on which to embark on any undertaking. As recently as the year 1745 Dean Swift wrote that 'Friday and Childermas are two cross days in the week, and it is impossible to have good luck on either of them'. In 1602

Pieter Brueghel (1525–69). The Massacre of the Innocents. c.1567.
Detail from the painting in the *Kunsthistorisches Museum, Vienna*.

The Martyrdom of St Thomas. Illumination in Manuscript Psalter, c. 1195. *British Museum.*

Richard Carew, Sheriff of Cornwall, pointed out that few things were as 'ominous as the beginning of a voyage on the day when Childermas fell'. It is said that Louis XVI of France would never transact business on it, and when Edward IV of England learned that the day had been chosen for his coronation he insisted on its postponement.

Many whipping customs used to be practised on this day—survivals of pre-Christian times. These were not concerned with punishment, but were intended to drive out harmful influences or convey by contact the virtues of a sacred tree.

The Fourth Day, 29 December, commemorates—like the First Day —a martyrdom. On this day, in 1644, John Evelyn was in Rome and wrote: 'We were invited by the English Jesuites to dinner being their greate fest of Tho: of Canterbury: We din'd in their common Refectory, and afterwards saw an Italian Comedy Acted by their Alumini before the Cardinals.'

Thomas à Becket, though he has no direct connexion with our Christmas feast, was the central figure in the grim tragedy at Canterbury at Christmastide 1170, an event of considerable importance in British history. For centuries pilgrims streamed in their thousands to do homage at his shrine.

He was born in 1118 on 21 December, the son of Gilbert Becket, a prosperous merchant and Sheriff of London. As a young man he was out hunting when his hawk stooped at a duck, and struck the water. Thomas leaped in to save it. The strong current dragged him downstream, and he would have been drowned if at that moment the mill wheel had not stopped and so saved his life. He regarded this as a miracle, that influenced him in his career, in which he became both Chancellor and Primate.

Every history-book tells something of his quarrel with King Henry II, and how the knights Reginald Fitzurse, William de Tracy, Hugh de Morville, and Richard le Breton came from France. Becket being in his cathedral, with a singularly poor-hearted band of his followers, the knights hung their cloaks on a mulberry tree, entered the building, and murdered him at the foot of the altar of St Benedict.

This death made Becket a European hero, and his cult brought great wealth to his shrine. Later, Henry VIII not only pillaged the shrine, but caused the saint to be cited that he should appear in court, and to be tried and condemned as a traitor, his name to be struck out of the calendar, and his bones to be burned and the ashes thrown to the air. There is indeed a poetic justice in the fact that four hundred years later Becket has been made the hero of immensely popular plays by two of the most notable playwrights of our time, T. S. Eliot and Anouilh.

*　　*　　*

The fourth day may be chosen as the centre, so to speak, of two very ancient Church customs that were spread over the days immediately following Christmas. The Feast of Fools was one—a series of disorderly revels among the lower ranking clergy and ministrants of the church. The services were burlesqued and the activities of the seniors mimicked: on occasion some inferior clerk sat upon a bishop's throne, perhaps hideously masked into the bargain. The lower clergy came from the peasant classes, and Sir E. K. Chambers described the feast as 'an ebullition of the natural lout beneath the cassock'—reviving a whole range of pagan customs still lying not very deep below the surface in the common man.

The Feast of Fools, with its abuses, was frequently attacked by Church reformers. It was prohibited in 1435 but was so popular that it lingered on for a century and a half, to be taken up by laymen outside the Church. This was in the form of organized revels in such quarters as the courts of the Tudor sovereigns, university colleges, and the large households of the nobility. They were presided over by the Lord of Misrule, who had been elected with much ceremony. These festivities were naturally disliked by the early Puritans, and we can turn to one of them, Philip Stubbes, for a description—taken from his *Anatomie of Abuses* (1585):

> First of all the wilde heades of the parishe conventynge together, chuse them a grand Capitaine (of mischeefe) whom they innoble with the title of my *Lorde of Misserule*, and hym they crown with great solemnitie, and adopt for their kyng. The kyng anoynted, chuseth for the twentie, fourtie, three score, or a hundred lustie guttes like to hymself, to wait uppon his lordely majestie, and to

guard his noble persone. Then every one of these his menne he investeth with his liveries of greene, yellowe or some other light wanton colour. And as though that were not baudie enough I should saie, they bedecke themselves with scarffes, ribbons, and laces, hanged all over with golde rynges, precious stones and other jewelles: This doen, they tye about either legge twentie or fourtie belles with rich handkercheefes in their handes, and sometimes laied acrosse over their shoulders and neckes, borrowed for the most part of their pretie Mopsies and loovying Bessies, for bussying them in the darcke. Thus thinges sette in order, they have their hobbie horses, dragons and other antiques, together with their baudie pipers, and thunderyng drommers, to strike up the Deville's Dance withall, then march these heathen companie towards the churche and churche yard, their pipers pipying, drommers thonderyng, their stumppes dauncying, their belles iynglyng, their handkerchiefes swyngyng about their heades like madmen, their hobbie horses and other monsters skyrmishyng amongst the throng: and in this sorte they go to the churche (though the minister bee at praier or preachyng) dauncying and swingying their handkercheefes over their heades, in the churche, like devilles incarnate, with suche a confused noise that no man can here his owene voice. Then the foolishe people, they looke, they stare, they laugh, they fleere, and mount upon formes and pewes, to see these goodly pageauntes, solemnized in this sort.

Older than the Feast of Fools were the Christmas revels of the deacons, the priests, and the choirboys, each held on a separate day. The most important of them was the Boy's Festival. Whereas the Fool's Feasts were largely Continental, the Boy's Festivals were popular in Britain. The choirboys elected from among themselves a Boy Bishop with his attendant dean, archdeacons, and so on. He was often given a dinner and then took part in a cavalcade. He preached a sermon. The ceremony was in the nature of a holiday, kept within bounds by the authorities, who approved of it. The actual election generally took place on St Nicholas's Day, 6 December; it culminated, and the ceremonies above were carried out, at Childermas. In a modified form the custom has lately been revived by enterprising clergy.

We have searched the works of the calendarians in vain for any event or circumstance that might connect the Fifth Day with the Feast of Christmas. Yet, we observe, the Christmas season is the time for ghost stories, and we have not yet told one. This would seem the moment for a passing glance at Borley Rectory, the 'most haunted house in England'.

It is perhaps significant that Borley Rectory was burnt down just after Christmas 1938. It is not so generally known that the fire was foretold by a *planchette* which was being operated by one of the late Harry Price's observers in Borley Rectory exactly one year earlier.

Harry Price described many strange occurrences at the Rectory, and one which is representative of many happened soon after Christmas, when he and another of his ghost-hunters were keeping watch in the old study, which Price called the 'Base Room'. Here is Harry Price's account of what they observed:

> After tea on that early January afternoon my friend and I prepared to settle down and await darkness—and what darkness might bring. The Oxford man sat at the table and began reading a newspaper. I was stretched full length on the camp-bed and I might have been about to drop off into a doze. The door of the Base Room was wide open in order that any sound above-stairs could be heard by us. It was a very still afternoon, with a Scotch mist outside, and everything was absolutely quiet in this exceptionally quiet Essex backwater.
>
> Just about five o'clock, when it was quite dark in the Base Room, my friend lit the oil lamp in order that he could continue his reading. He was sitting near the door, and I was still reclining on the camp-bed. He had hardly picked up his newspaper again, when we were startled by the sound of three short, sharp raps, repeated three times, which appeared to come from the Base Room door, which was in full view of, and quite near, my friend. The Oxford boy was a tyro at ghost-hunting and it rather unnerved him for a moment. *He* could see there was nothing at or near the door. I sat up on the bed.
>
> We waited a minute or so for a repetition of the raps. As these were not forthcoming, I jumped off the bed with the intention of exploring the passage leading to the Base Room. I had hardly crossed the room when both of us heard loud footsteps traversing the passage outside the room. They appeared to be passing our door. Before we

had recovered from our surprise—if I can use so mild a term—a door slammed in the back part of the house, near the kitchen quarters.

We rushed out of the Base Room and down the long passage which led to the kitchen, but found nothing disturbed. We had carefully noted the position of each door, and none had been moved by so much as a hairbreadth. All our seals were intact and no one could have entered or left the house without our knowledge. At least, no tangible being could have done so. With our torches we then searched the whole house from attics to cellars without finding anything that would account for the almost incredible noises—incredible under the circumstances—which we had heard. There is a French proverb to the effect that a ghost was never seen by two pairs of eyes; but two pairs of ears undoubtedly heard the raps on the door and the footsteps. And there was nothing ambiguous about the slamming of that door.

On the Sunday evening after Borley Rectory was burnt down a young man from Long Melford, with his girl friend, visited the rectory to look at the ruins. They made their way to the back of the house where the best view of the damage could be obtained. It was full moon, and a bright, still evening. Although all the upper part of Borley Rectory was burnt out, the brick gable ends were still standing. In the centre of the house was a gable which once contained the window of the Blue Room—a bedroom which figures largely in all accounts of the manifestations at Borley. As the two young people gazed at the charred ruins in the moonlight, they saw a girl, dressed in white (or very pale blue), lean out of the Blue Room window—or what remained of it—and then fall back amongst the burnt rafters. Harry Price declared that he had interviewed both the young man and his girl and both were unshaken in their conviction that they saw the apparition, which was perfectly visible for several seconds.

Since this is the season for startling stories, and we are approaching Hogmanay, this may also be the right occasion to call upon that great Scottish 'poet and tragedian', William McGonagall, for a contribution. McGonagall, a Dundee handloom weaver, born in 1830, had an unrivalled and irrepressible gift for celebrating great events—the more spectacular and tragic the better. It is doubtful if this master of bathos ever found a worthier subject for his impetuous pen than the Tay Bridge disaster, which, as he tells us more than once, occurred 'On the last Sabbath day of 1879'.

'Twas about seven o'clock at night,
And the wind it blew with all its might,
And the rain came pouring down,
And the dark clouds seem'd to frown,
And the Demon of the air seem'd to say—
'I'll blow down the Bridge of Tay.'

When the train left Edinburgh
The passengers' hearts were light and felt no sorrow,
But Boreas blew a terrific gale,
Which made the hearts for to quail,
And many of the passengers with fear did say—
'I hope God will send us safe across the Bridge of Tay' . . .

So the train sped on with all its might,
And Bonnie Dundee soon hove in sight,
And the passengers' hearts felt light,
Thinking they would enjoy themselves on the New Year,
With their friends at home they lov'd most dear,
And wish them all a happy New Year.

So the train mov'd slowly along the Bridge of Tay,
Until it was about midway,
Then the central girders with a crash gave way
And down went the train and the passengers into the Tay!
The Storm Fiend did loudly bray,
Because ninety lives had been taken away,
On the last Sabbath day of 1879,
Which will be remember'd for a very long time . . .

It must have been an awful sight,
To witness in the dusky moonlight
While the Storm Fiend did laugh, and angry did bray,
Along the Railway Bridge of the Silvr'y Tay,
Oh' ill-fated Bridge of the Silvr'y Tay,
I must now conclude my lay,
By telling the world fearlessly without the least dismay,
That your central girders would not have given way,
At least many sensible men do say,
Had they been supported on each side with buttresses,
At least many sensible men confesses,
For the stronger we our houses do build,
The less chance we have of being killed.

Fortunately the Storm Fiend seldom 'brays' to such disastrous effect, but the turn of the year usually brings seasonable snow and frost, and skating is traditionally the chief outdoor recreation of the last days of Christmastide. Skating, however, was a novelty in England when Pepys

and Evelyn both watched it on the new canal in St James's Park in 1662. When the ice was breaking up, just before Christmas, Pepys was worried by the Duke of York's foolhardiness: 'Though the ice was broken dangerous, yet he would go slide upon his scates, which I did not like, but he slides very well.'

The royal family had learned to skate while they were in exile in Holland. Thenceforth skating became a fashionable and elegant exercise in England, and one which gained in popularity during the famous frost of 1684, when a fair was held on the frozen Thames (which was to inspire, 250 years later, a marvellous description of skating in the pages of Virginia Woolf's *Orlando*). Frost fairs were also held in 1715–16, 1739–40, 1789, and 1814.

The adoption of curved skates, shorter and higher than the long

runners depicted in Dutch paintings of the seventeenth century, en-
couraged the art of figure-skating in England during the eighteenth
century, an art which was codified by Lieutenant Robert Jones in his
Treatise on Skating in 1772. The popularity of the various editions of
this work no doubt accounted for the outcrop of skating prints and
caricatures towards the end of the century.

Considering its æsthetic as well as its athletic appeal, skating has a
curiously scanty literature. James Thomson, in *The Seasons* (1730), has
a few lines about it, but Wordsworth's famous passage in *The Prelude*
is almost the only poetic tribute which rises worthily to the theme. It
is perhaps significant that Wordsworth, even at the age of sixty, was
regarded as the crack skater on Rydal; and an old man of the district
is recorded by Canon Rawnsley as saying: 'He was a ter'ble girt skater
was Wudsworth now. He would stand up straight and swaay and swing
away grandly.'

The correspondence of skating with dancing was noted at the outset
by Lieutenant Jones, in his *Treatise*. And, just as dancing can be an
expression of love, so can skating.

The amorous connotations of skating are exquisitely depicted by
Adam Buck in his 'Skating Lovers', of which the original drawing may
still exist somewhere, but which is known to us only in the lovely
coloured aquatint of it made in 1800 by Roberts and Stadler. This is a
perfect illustration of some lines written over a hundred years later by
E. B. Osborn:

> She flies, I follow. Thus her power I own
> That am her poor, obsequious shadow grown—
> For still I touch her, still I'm left alone!
>
> She flies, I follow. Though her finger-tips
> Are all I hold, yet at her unseen lips
> My soul flits on before, and bee-like sips.
>
> She flies, I follow. Hear the dulcet chime
> Of steel on ice that marks the magic time,
> And breaks the rhythmic silence as with rhyme!

Adam Buck (fl. 1795–1834). Skating Lovers. Aquatint by Piercy Roberts and J. C. Stadler. 1800. *British Museum*.

W. B. Murray. New Year's Eve in Canongate, Edinburgh, 1876. Engraving.

12

Hogmanay

It is important to differentiate between the customs that pertain strictly to this day and those preliminaries that merely serve to while away the time until the clock strikes midnight and the calendar is changed. Even so, the world is so spread over with Scots that their ceremony, Hogmanay, though it fails by less than a second in falling into the New Year, must be accorded first place.

Scotland, it has been said, is—or perhaps one should now say *was*—the most Protestant part of Europe. Puritanism and the old Christmas celebrations were bad bed-fellows, and Old Christmas was long ago shown the door. We cannot help thinking, however, that he gets his own back on New Year's Day.

Hogmanay is the eve of the great occasion, and drinking is a great feature of its celebration. The word itself, found in varying forms in Scotland and northern England, is of obscure origin. It has affinities with words found in rhymes connected with old New Year customs in parts of France, such as *hoguinana*.

In 1893 Hogmanay in Edinburgh was described as follows:

> Towards evening the thoroughfares become thronged with the youth of the city. . . . As the midnight hour approaches, drinking of healths becomes more frequent, and some are already intoxicated. . . . The eyes of the immense crowd are ever being turned towards the lighted clock-face of 'Auld and Faithfu' Tron (Church), the hour approaches, the hands seem to stand still, but in one second more the hurrahing, and cheering, the hand-shaking, the health-drinking, is all kept up as long as the clock continues to ring out the much-longed-for midnight hour. . . .
> The crowds slowly disperse, the much intoxicated and helpless

ones being hustled about a good deal, the police urging them on out of harm's way. The first-footers are off. . . .

But we have already passed our moment of demarcation into the New Year and must return to New Year's Eve. As is not unusual, on the eve of a festival, some of the customs are in the nature of charms. In England, Scotland, Wales, and Italy there were variations of a 'new water' charm. Last thing on New Year's Eve water was drawn from the well in a manner prescribed by rituals. It was drunk on the next day as a charm against witchcraft and similar displeasing afflictions.

Processions of various kinds—noise and rowdiness being a common denominator—were once a feature of New Year's Eve. Robert Chambers prints what he calls a *restored* (by memory) version of a song sung by processioners in Orkney; the Queen Mary referred to is the Virgin:

> This night it is guid New-r E'ens night,
>   We're a' here, Queen Mary's men;
> And we're come here to crave our right,
>   And that's before our Lady.

> The very first thing which we do crave,
>   We're a' here, Queen Mary's men;
> A bonny white cradle we must have,
>   And that's before our Lady.

> Goodwife, gae to your butter-ark,
> And weigh us here ten mark.

> Ten mark, ten pound,
> Look that ye grip weel to the grund
> Good wife, gae to your geelin vat,
> And fetch us here a skeel of that.
> Gang to your awmrie, gin ye please,
> And bring frae there a yow-milk cheese.

> And syne bring here a sharping stane,
> We'll sharp our whittles ilka ane.
> Ye'll cut the cheese, and eke the round,
> But aye take care ye cutna your thoom.
> Gae fill the three-pint cog o' ale,
> The maut maun be aboon the meal.

We houp your ale is stark and stout,
For men to drink the auld year owt.

Ye ken the weather's snow and sleet,
Stir up the fire to warm our feet.
Our shoon's made o' mares skin,
Come open the door and let us in.

The party then rushed into the house, where they were handsomely
fed. They then went on to the next one. Drinking the old year out, it
scarcely need be said, is very much less common than drinking the new
one in.

In Scotland, juniper was burned in the house to protect the inmates
—human and animal—from harm; in Catholic Germany and Austria
this was replaced by the rather more pleasant scent of incense and holy
water. In Scotland, too, it was once important to drive stray dogs from
the premises. But these dogs were nothing like so fearsome as those described by Marie Trevelyan as being active in Wales on New Year's Eve:

> The Cwn Annwn are celebrated as spirit-hounds passing through
> the air in pursuit of objects of their malice, and their howling was
> regarded as an omen of death. These dogs have been variously
> described. Sometimes they appear as very small dogs, white as the
> drifted snow, with tiny ears quite rose-coloured inside, and eyes
> that glittered like brilliant moonbeams. In some parts of Wales
> they are described as being black and very ugly, with huge red
> spots, or red in body, with large black patches like splashes of ink.
> The most terrible of these spirit-hounds were said to be of a
> blood-red colour, and when seen were dripping with gore, while
> their eyes resembled balls of liquid fire. In some places they were
> known as small liver-coloured dogs, all 'Spots and spangles' of
> red and white, or flame coloured.

In Greece children sing carols in honour of St Basil, Bishop of
Cæsarea, preacher and doctor, who died on 1 January in 379. Christians
of the Orthodox Church still celebrate his festival on that day (Old
Style) though the Roman Catholics recall him on 14 June, the traditional
date of his consecration. It is, however, on New Year's Eve in modern
Greece, but nowhere else, that processions of singers go from house to

house making collections, with the usual good wishes to the inmates.

One song they sing records how the saint as a boy came down from Cæsarea, bearing pen and ink. When he is challenged, he replies that he is on his way from his home to school. 'Then say the A.B.C. . . .' he is asked. His staff, as he leans upon it to recite the alphabet, begins to sprout: soon partridges and pigeons come to perch in its branches. Moreover, the pigeons bring in their claws water from the cold fountains, and on their wings snow, to bathe the master and mistress of the visited household. The theme then rather surprisingly changes:

> O lady tall, O lady fine,
> With eyebrows of the silken twine,
> Lady, when on a holiday
> You dress for church in best array,
> Then for your face the Sun you don,
> And for your breast the Moon put on
> And on your finger gleaming far
> Is set the lovely Morning Star.

> We have sung enough my Lady's praise,
> Now for my Lord your voices raise.
> O Lord and Master, five times o'er,
> Five times again, and five times more,
> Feel in your pocket broiderèd,
> Your pocket worked with silver thread,
> And if you find piastres there,
> Give them to us and do not spare—
> Or pounds or silver buttons give
> Them all to us, that you may live.
> And many happy returns of the day.

Thomas Hardy recorded the old Wessex celebrations on the Eve:

> Our songs went up and out the chimney,
> And roused the home-gone husbandmen;
> Our allemands, our heys, pousettings,
> Our hands-across and back again,
> Sent rhythmic throbbings through the casements
>   On to the white highway,
> Where nighted farers paused and muttered,
>   'Keep it up well, do they!'

First-Footing in Edinburgh. Engraving from Chambers's *Book of Days*, 1863.

Thomas Packer (fl. 1850–1900). Lithograph for the cover of 'The Chimes Polka', by Henry Farmer. c. 1880.

◇◆◇◆◇◆◇◆◇◆◇◆◇◆◇◆◇◆◇◆◇◆◇◆◇◆◇◆◇◆◇◆◇◆◇◆◇◆◇

> The contrabasso's measured booming
> Sped at each bar to the parish bounds,
> To shepherds at their midnight lambings,
> To stealthy poachers on their rounds;
> And everybody caught full duly
> The notes of our delight,
> As Time unrobed the Youth of Promise
> Hailed by our sanguine sight.

The poem, it will be recalled, goes on to compare this simple behaviour with that on New Year's Eve during the 1914–18 war. But to most
of us, as the years pass, it is not so much the customs and celebrations
that concern us, but consideration of the past and anticipation of the
future—a mingling of melancholy and optimism. This mood, we think,
has been caught by none better than the gentle and now unwisely
neglected Elia:

Every man hath two birthdays; two days at least, in every year
which set him upon revolving the lapse of time, as it affects his
mortal duration. The one is that which in an especial manner he
termeth his. In the gradual desuetude of old observances, this
custom of solemnizing our proper birthday hath nearly passed
away, or is left to children, who reflect nothing at all about the
matter, nor understand anything in it beyond cake and orange.
But the birth of a New Year is of an interest too wide to be pre-
termitted by king or cobbler. No one ever regarded the First of
January with indifference. It is that from which all date their time,
and count upon what is left. It is the nativity of our common
Adam.
    Of all sound of all bells—(bells, the music nighest bordering
upon heaven)—most solemn and touching is the peal which rings
out the Old Year. I never hear it without a gathering-up of my
mind to a concentration of all the images that have been diffused
over the past twelvemonth; all I have done or suffered, performed or
neglected—in that regretted time. I begin to know its worth, as when
a person dies. It takes a personal colour; nor was it a poetical flight
in a contemporary, when he exclaimed—
    I saw the skirts of the departing Year.

13

New Year's Day

And when eight days were accomplished for the circumcising of
the child, his name was called Jesus, which was so named of the
angel before he was conceived in the womb.

So does the Gospel of the day, taken from St Luke, conclude. Yet it is
undeniable that almost all the traditions and customs that have been
associated with the first day of the year descend from ancient pre-
Christian festivals. We have seen that some of the practices of the Roman
Kalends have become attached to Christmas; likewise Celtic and Teutonic
traditions which must have belonged to December have been moved
to the first day of January, which, in our modern calendar, coincides
with Rome's New Year Day.

The connexion between Rome and this day is a close one. The
month is named after the Roman god Janus, who had two faces looking
in opposite directions, because, said the Latin grammarian Macrobius,
this month might be considered retrospective to the past and prospec-
tive to the opening year. The link is again to be found in countries where
it is the custom to exchange visits and to give presents on New Year's
Day in addition, or even as an alternative, to Christmas Day. In America,
the visiting—which became riotous, often with heavy drinking—was at
one time universal. But it has now largely died out. In Britain, New Year's
gifts on a lavish scale, particularly to the sovereign—Elizabeth I was a
very fortunate beneficiary—were usual until Jacobean times.

The Church had no scruples in making use of these pagan traditions
as symbols of the New Year, and they are sometimes to be found represented in medieval church carvings. At Worle in Somerset is a two-
headed Janus-like man, and at Malvern a figure holds a glass in each
hand, one to drink to the old, the other to the New Year.

On the Continent New Year's Day is observed with present-giving in several countries. It is so in Germany. Particularly in France does the connexion with the Roman Kalends remain. The French name for presents, *étrennes*, is derived directly from *strenae*, the Roman gifts of the New Year. The following account from Paris printed in the *Illustrated London News* of 7 January 1860 shows how different was the practice of celebration from that in northern Europe. The illustration, which we reproduce opposite page 148, was drawn by M. Beauce.

In order to give opportunities for an ample provision of presents to suit all purses, not only do the principal shops make an extra display towards the end of the old year, but permission is given for a fortnight to a considerable number of little merchants to erect stalls in the greatest thoroughfares. The great boulevards, from the Madeleine to the Bastille, are thus converted into a double line of tastefully-arranged bazaars, in which those pretty articles for which Paris is so celebrated abound. If the weather prove favourable, as it has done this year, these brief speculations turn out advantageously.

The pilgrims of the boulevards return from them with a load of toys and sweetmeats designed for speedy distribution; Punches or Polichinelles protrude from their pockets, drums hang corpulently from their waists, and the passage through The Needles is not more critical than the safe arrival of their acquisitions at the homes of the purchasers. Our view of 'The Boulevards' is a little section of the Boulevard des Italiens. . . .

A great number of minor receptions and felicitations are held and offered on the eve of the New Year, in order to give certain persons the opportunity of attending the most important ceremony of the fete, which takes place at the Imperial Palace, and is represented in our engraving as the 'Reception at the Tuileries'. The Emperor, surrounded by all the great dignitaries of the Empire, 'receives' the complimentary visits of the corps d'état, the Ambassadors, the Marshals of France, Generals, Ec. The same ceremony *in petto* is gone through by the different Ministers, who 'receive' their employees; by the large manufacturers and tradesmen, who 'receive' their workmen and servants, who expect to 'receive' in return the usual *gratification*, or *étrenne*.

The sweet-meat palaces in Paris have at all times been celebrated, and at this period of the year are inundated by visitors; so much so that on New-Year's eve they are difficult of access, and generally keep open all night. The best toyshops are in a similar state of siege; and the customers vie with each other in the acquisition of the tasteful objects submitted to their choice in some of the greatest establishments in Paris, such as that of M. Giroux represented in our illustration.

In the English-speaking world, although the first day of January was popularly regarded as New Year's Day, the year did not officially start then until 1752, when the Act was passed altering the mode of reckoning time from the Julian to the Gregorian style. Some reckonings, however, including the British fiscal year, remained unchanged, and they still begin on the old Lady Day, which became 6 April.

A very widely held tradition is that of first-footing. It is based on the belief that the character of the first person to enter a household in the New Year affects its welfare. The custom is particularly strong in Scotland and with Scots all over the world. It used to be considered essential for the luck of a household that the first person to enter after midnight should bear gifts of cake and bread and cheese, of which every member should eat.

Early in the last century the principal streets of Edinburgh were so thronged with first-footers that between midnight and one o'clock there were more people about than was usual at midday. It was said that 'much innocent mirth prevailed and material good feeling promoted'— possibly because all drank from the 'hot pint', a flagon of warm, spiced, and sweetened ale with an infusion of spirits. After about 1812 the custom fell away because youths, well organized into gangs, attacked and robbed those persons with white neck-cloths because it was likely that they would be carrying valuables, and, of course, because they were easily picked out in the dark. The Frenchman Louis Simon, in his *Journal of a Tour and Residence in Great Britain*, wrote rather acidly:

Jan. 1. 1811. There is no sleeping the first night of the year at Edinburgh. It is a received custom for the common people to give a kiss to any woman in the streets, about midnight, on foot, or in carriages. Few women expose themselves to this rude salutation.

New Year's Day at Paris. Engraving in the *Illustrated London News*,
6 January, 1860.

John Collet (1725–80). Winter. c.1770. Hand-coloured engraving
printed by Carington Bowles. *British Museum*.

But the streets are full, notwithstanding, of unruly boys, who knock at house doors, and make a noise all night. This is a little relic of the coarse manners of former times, which is still tolerated; and considering what this country was before its union with England, there is, perhaps, more reason to be astonished at the advanced state of its police than otherwise.

There has always been some controversy about the qualifications that give a first-footer the desirable potency. Should he be dark or fair? In an attempt to secure enlightenment on this, a correspondent signing himself Prestoniensis wrote to *Notes and Queries* of 25 October 1856, recalling that for many years past he had been in the habit of calling on a friend, an aged lady, at an early hour on New Year's Day, this being by her own desire, as he was a fair-complexioned person, and therefore assumed to be of good omen for the events of the year. On one occasion he was prevented from fulfilling his old friend's request, and her first caller proved to be a dark-complexioned man; in consequence that year brought sickness, trouble, and commercial disaster. 'Can any of your readers,' Prestoniensis asked, 'tell me if this preference for fair-visaged folk is general?' We have searched *Notes and Queries* in vain for a reply; no one, it seems, dared an answer to this important question. One thing, however, seems to be undisputed: any female first-footer would inevitably bring ill luck.

There are many variations of the first-footing theme. A correspondent informed the readers of *Notes and Queries* in 1875 that in the Teme Valley, and no doubt other places in the west country, boys still went round the houses of the villages—and in Worcester itself—before daylight singing songs; one of them would then be admitted into the kitchen 'for good luck all the year', and halfpence distributed to the band. In the same districts it was customary, as an avoidance of ill luck, to postpone washing day should it fall on New Year's Day. Many persons, too, were convinced that it was most unlucky to receive a gift of new shoes on that day.

We have already referred to 'new water' drawn from the wells on New Year's Eve. A writer from South Wales described such a custom in *The Athenaeum* of 5 February 1848. Children drew water early on New Year's Day and, carrying it around in a jug, sprinkled it with a spray of some evergreen upon all whom they met, wishing them a happy New Year. They would also serenade households with the following song:

> Here we bring new water
>   From the well so clear,
> For to worship God with,
>   This happy New Year.
> Sing levy-dew, sing levy-dew,
>   The water and the wine;
> The seven bright gold wires
>   And the bugles they do shine.
>
> Sing reign of Fair Maid,
>   With gold upon her toe—
> Open you the West Door,
>   And turn the old Year go:
> Sing reign of Fair Maid,
>   With gold upon her chin—
> Open you the East Door,
>   And let the New Year in.

The writer adds that this was sung in English, and he recorded the words just as they were sung. He suggests that 'levy dew' might be *Levez, Dieu,* and wonders if the 'Fair Maid' may be Aurora or the Virgin, and if it should be *reine* rather than 'reign'.

In general, New Year's Day superstitions tend to be on the lines that if you begin the year well so it will continue. Avoid, for example, anything of ill omen; have plenty of money in your pocket on the first day, or dine well if you would have plenty to eat in the ensuing year. This may be the reason for a feast described in *The Gentleman's Magazine* of 1811, when, on 1 January, the chief magistrate of Cheshire, General Grosvenor, gave a most sumptuous entertainment in the Exchange to his cousin, Earl Grosvenor, several gentlemen of the county, the corporation, and his friends in the city, of whom two hundred sat down to dine at five o'clock.

The town hall was decorated with variegated lamps. On the centre table was placed a baron of beef ornamented with appropriate devices and encircled by the motto 'O! the roast beef of old England, O! the English roast beef!' On its right was a pie weighing upwards of 200 lbs. containing four geese, four turkeys, six hares, a leg of veal, a leg of pork, sausages, etcetera, carrying on its sides the heraldic bearings of the house of Eaton and those of the general. By its side was a salad, tastefully displayed, with the motto: 'Prosperity to the Trade of Chester'.

Among the other items that they tackled in addition to the beef, the pie, and the salad, were sixteen tureens of turtle soup, twelve roast and boiled turkeys together with ten haunches and ten necks of venison. The meal concluded with thirty salvers of whips and jellies, twenty jelly moulds, as well as blancmanges, tarts, cheese-cakes, mince-pies, and puffs. Possibly, on the following morning, the prospects for the coming year seemed a little less bright.

In the eighteenth century a feature of the New Year was the composition and delivery of an Ode by the Poet Laureate. The royal family assembled on New Year's Day to listen to this seasonal verse, recited and sung to music. Colley Cibber's Odes, and those of William Whitehead, his successor, were thus performed. Cibber's annual poems, produced from 1730 to 1757, were so bad that his friends were driven to affirm that he made them so on purpose.

It is pleasing to go back five centuries to the freshness of a poem translated from the manuscript of Benedictbeuren, the famous medieval anthology, by Helen Waddell, called simply 'New Year'. We quote the opening verses:

> New Year has brought renewing, winter's gone,
> Short daylight lengthens and the winds are still,
> The year's first month of January's here,
> And in my mind the tides still ebb and flow.
> For a girl's sake.
>
> Slenderly fashioned is she, wise and fair,
> Lovelier than the lily or the rose.
> The Queen of France is not so beautiful.
> And Death is now near neighbour unto me
> Unless she heal the wound she made in me.
> Flower o' the thorn.

14

From the Eighth Day to the Tenth

On the eighth day the calendar again fails to provide us with anything to commemorate; but this is an appropriate opportunity to consider the cult of the Christmas party—other than the traditional family gathering on Christmas Day. Since the coming of better roads and easier transport in the early days of the last century, the two weeks following Christmas have been the occasion for parties of all kinds, from those arranged while children are home from school to the 'works parties' which bring so much business to the catering trade, the dance bands, and theatrical managements. To these we must add Christmas conversaziones held by learned bodies at which professors and the *cognoscenti* combine displays of their learning with the eating of ice-creams and trifles. This has become the season, also, for lectures which provide cultural or scientific information for the young in what is assumed to be entertaining form.

The social historian has not, apparently, studied these phenomena, amongst which the children's party—surely a nineteenth century introduction—is outstanding. It has lately acquired lustre, tinged with the shadow of dread, in the poems of John Betjeman.

That children's parties were still novel in the eighteen-forties is apparent from the writings of Thackeray. He was constrained to address *A Remonstrance Concerning Them* to Mr Punch:

> The awful spread of Juvenile Parties, sir, is the fact to which I would draw your attention. There is no end to those entertainments, and if the custom be not speedily checked, people will be obliged to fly from London at Christmas and hide their children during the holidays....

As a first step towards remedying the evil Thackeray asks Mr Punch to consider his own responsibility for it:

> You, sir, have by your agents, caused not a little of the mischief. I desire that, during Christmas time at least, Mr Leech shall be abolished, or sent to take a holiday. Judging from his sketches, I should say that he must be endowed with a perfectly monstrous organ of philoprogenitiveness; he revels in the delineation of the dearest and most beautiful little boys and girls in turn-down collars, and broad sashes, and produces in your *Almanack* a picture of a child's costume ball, in which he has made the little wretches in the dresses of every age, and looking so happy, beautiful, and charming, that I have carefully kept the picture from the sight of the women and children of my own household, and—I will not say burned it, for I had not the heart to do that—but locked it away privately, lest they should conspire to have a costume ball themselves, and little Polly should insist on appearing in the address of Anne Boleyn, or little Jacky upon turning out as an Ancient Briton.

Thackeray objects strongly to the portrayal of a children's ball as if it were a sort of Paradise, and the little imps engaged as happy and pretty as so many cherubs. They should, he writes, be drawn:

> as hideous—disagreeable—distorted—affected—jealous of each other—dancing awkwardly—with shoes too tight for them—over-eating themselves at supper—very unwell (and deservedly so) the next morning, with Mamma administering a mixture made after the Doctor's prescription, and which shall be painted awfully black, in an immense large teacup, and (as might be shown by the horrible expression on the little patient's face) of the most disgusting flavour.

However, he has a good word or two for that favourite entertainment of his time, the magic lantern show:

> I still sometimes get a degree of pleasure by hearing the voices of children in the dark, and the absurd remarks which they make as the various scenes are presented—as, in the dissolving views, Cornhill changes into Grand Cairo, as Cupid comes down with a wreath, and pops it on to the head of the Duke of Wellington, as St Peter's

at Rome suddenly becomes illuminated, and fireworks, not the least like real fireworks, begin to go off from Fort St Angelo—it is certainly not unpleasant to hear the 'o–o–o's' of the audience, and the little children chattering in the darkness.

Today the Magic Lantern, in the form of the projector of colour transparencies, is even more ubiquitous at Christmas entertainments than it was in Thackeray's time. There seems to be some doubt as to the precise details of the invention of this device, which happened in the late seventeenth century. In 1696 there was described 'a certain small Optical Macheen, that shews by a gloomy light upon a white wall, Spectres and Monsters so hideous that he who knows not the Secret, believes it to be performed by Magick Art'.

That the Magic Lantern was in common use as a domestic entertainment in the early part of the eighteenth century is shown by a minor poet, Henry Travers, who included in his *Miscellaneous Poems and Translations*, published in 1731, a poem entitled 'The Magic Lantern', which was stated to be 'translated from the Latin of Mr Titley'. Allowing for differences in subject-matter, which are accountable to the taste of the period, the 'magic' provided by 'the thin creation of delusive art' appears to have been just as effective as it was in Thackeray's day or our own schooldays:

> Expand the sportive Scene, the Lantern show,
> No gleam of Day must thro' the Darkness glow;
> The fleeting Forms abhor the envious Light,
> Love the brown Shade, and only live by Night . . .
> See thro' the Gloom the fiery Splendor fall;
> Glares the red Lens around the dusky wall.

The images projected by Mr Travers's or Mr Titley's Magic Lantern included 'satire shapes', each of which 'grins horribly a ghastly Smile', sceptred monarchs, 'blooming Maids in beauteous Lustre', knights and dragons, Bacchus, a 'lifeless skull . . . emblem of dreary Death', and 'a horrid ghost', calculated to cause the viewer to

> Bewail your lonely Bed with wild Affright,
> And dread the lengthen'd Horrors of the Night.

THE MAGIC LANTERN

After the lurid descriptions of this 'baleful Sprite' it is with some relief that one reaches the closing lines of the poem and the end of the performance:

> Now let the Splendor of returning Light
> Strike thro' the artificial Shades of Night;
> Lo the strong Flame the airy Phantoms shun,
> Fade in the Blaze, and die before the Sun.

In the latter part of the next century the Magic Lantern was used by the Savoyards strolling about Europe to amuse ignorant people. In the nineteenth century much ingenuity was brought to the design of slides: men in bed would be seen swallowing an endless succession of rats, and moving geometrical designs in bright colours would weave unending patterns. Then came photography and its marvels. The hissing lime light, with its cylinders of compressed gas, was replaced by the blinding electric arc.

The adult parties of Christmastide reached their hey-day at the time of the amateur ballad singer. And the vogue for 'drawing room music' of all kinds, not merely sentimental ballads about love, parting, and bereavement, but also jolly polkas, waltzes, Lancers, and quadrilles, created one of the most charming minor art forms of the nineteenth century—the coloured music cover, designed and lithographed by such engaging *genre* artists as Concanen, Brandard, and Packer. Sometimes these delightful designs express not merely the essential æsthetic flavour of the period but also—as in Packer's cover for 'The Chimes Polka'—the strange incongruities of Christmastide sentiment.

By 1866 Christmas parties had become so numerous, indeed universal, that Dr R. W. Dale felt called upon to discuss the morality of the subject in its widest terms in the *Sunday Magazine*:

> Would it not be possible to try whether the conversation of our Christmas parties might not be playful, cheerful and even merry, and yet not altogether frivolous and useless? There would be the advantage, at least, in giving religious people a chance of talking about religion—the conversation would assume a higher intellectual character. They know more, and think more, about religion

than most subjects, except their families and their business. They are more interested in religious truth than in any other truth. If once they could speak about it freely, they would speak their best. Anyhow, might not certain forms of Christian work be talked of when Christian men meet together? Are not the difficulties of town missions at least as interesting as the blunders of town councils? Is not a ragged school as good a subject of conversation as a new system of drainage? Would not the prospects of Christianity in India be as pleasant a topic of speculation as the future of the Italian kingdom? May not the condition of the poor of the neighbourhood suggest a more manly as well as a more Christian discussion than the movements of the Prince of Wales? Is not the annual report of a great hospital a better thing to talk about than the gossip of the *Court Journal*? Might not the ethics of common business be as interesting a subject as the history of the recent financial panic, and the chances of improvement in the shares of Joint-Stock Companies (Limited)?

Regretfully we observe that our conversational topics a hundred years later are largely unchanged by his exhortations.

'The Magic Lantern'. Coloured engraving from *Aunt Louisa's Toy Book*, c. 1867.

Victorian black-lacquered wall bracket painted with Christmastide scenes. Photograph by Edwin Smith. *Mrs. Mark Lubbock.*

15

The Eve of the Epiphany

The Eleventh Day, 5 January, is the Eve of the Epiphany, the manifestation of Christ to the Gentiles. It commemorates one of the great journeys of mythology, the coming to Bethlehem of the wise men from the East. To this hallowed and romantic Christian occasion, however, have been attached some decidedly earthy pagan observances, of which the one called in England 'wassailing' is perhaps the most long-lived.

Wassailing is a somewhat complicated rite, involving the drinking of toasts, which may originally have been intended as an offering to pagan spirits but became a sacramental act designed to fertilize and encourage the yield of fruit trees. It is a rite that occurred in varying forms on the Continent of Europe, and in some places on Christmas Eve or at other times during the Christmas season. In the Tyrol it took place on St Thomas's Eve, 21 December, when the Christmas pies were being made. The most usual occasion, however, at least in Britain, has always been on the evening before the Twelfth Day.

As still carried on in the south-west of England, the ceremony starts with the assembly of the farmer and his men at the foot of a favoured apple tree, carrying jugs of cider and their guns. They drink to this toast—or a variation of it:

> Here's to the old apple-tree
> Whence thou may'st bud, and whence thou may'st blow!
> And whence thou may'st bear apples enow!
> Hats full! Caps full!
> Bushel—bushel—sacks full,
> And my pockets full too! Huzza!

Then, as they cheer, they fire their guns into the tree.

At Haslemere in Surrey a rather similar toast used to be concluded, less dangerously, by three blasts on a horn. In Gloucestershire and Herefordshire wassailing used to be combined with a fire ceremony. *The Gentleman's Magazine* for 1753 carried the following communication; dated Hereford, 30 September:

> In your Magazine for January last I observed your correspondent A. B. and C. give a concise account of Wassailing. . . . As I have many years been an attendant on these social and hospitable meetings, permit me to offer to your readers some particulars of this ceremony, as I have seen it kept up, with all due form on the farm of *Huntington*, two miles West from Hereford, that for many years was occupied by my late respectable friend and neighbour, Mr Samuel Tully, well known to the publick and many of your readers, as a farmer and grazier. . . .
>
> On the eve of Twelfth-day (the Epiphany) Mr Tully and his numerous visitors, near the hour of six o'clock in the evening, walked to a field, and on the highest part of the land one large and twelve smaller fires were lighted up. While burning, the master and some of his company, formed in a circle round the larger fire, and after pledging each other in good Herefordshire cyder, all the attendants joined in shouting and rejoicing. On the fires being extinguished, the company all returned to the hospitable mansion, where an excellent and plentiful supper was provided for the family and all ranks of visitors. After the glass had circulated, and some songs had been sung, and happiness diffused through all the numerous company, near the hour of nine or ten o'clock, a second procession was formed, by all who joined in the concluding or more interesting ceremony. On coming to the outhouse, where the oxen and cows were in their stalls, the bailiff attended with a large plum-cake, which, when made, had a hole in the middle. Previous to its being placed on the horn of the ox, the master and his friends each took a small cup with ale, and drank a toast to each ox, in nearly the following words (each of the 24 oxen having a name): the master began with the first:

> *Here's to the Benbaw,* and to thy white horn,*
> *God send thy master a good crop of corn;*
> *You eat your oats, and I'll drink my beer;*
> *May the Lord send us all a happy new year!*

* The ox's name, a common one.

After the last ox was toasted, the bailiff placed the cake on the horn of the first ox, the boy touching him with a pointed goad. This induced the ox to shake his head, when the cake was tossed on either side; if on one side, it was to be the perquisite of the bailiff, who divided it amongst the company. On returning to the house, mirth and feasting prevailed till a late, or rather an early hour.

It is remarkable, and cannot be a coincidence, that there is or was a custom among the southern Slavs in which a Christmas cake with a hole in it was placed on the horn of the chief ox. In Wales, a similar ceremony with a holed cake was also performed, but with variations. It occurred on Christmas Eve, and it was a ceremony of prognostication: if the ox remained quiet, the omen was good; if restless, then bad luck would follow.

Dr Bull in *Herefordshire Pomona* writes that he remembered the bonfire ceremony as lately as 1879. A hawthorn bush was partly burned, and the unconsumed fragments were carried away to confer fertility on the fields.

In some countries it is on the Eve of the Epiphany that the first stages of the election of the Bean King are carried out. So it was in Lorraine during the last century, where the election was combined with an augury. The household and any guests assembled round the table, above which, centrally, was hung a lamp. The company looked to the walls, and anyone present whose shadow was not cast upon them could be sure that he or she would die within the year. That part of the ceremony safely concluded (we hope), the King of the feast, who had previously been chosen by the drawing of lots, chose his Queen. They were given the place of honour, and each time they raised their glasses to drink, cries of 'The King drinks! the Queen drinks!' came from all around. (The more conventional form of choosing the Bean King of Epiphany, however, occurred on the Twelfth Day.)

These pagan survivals, though they enjoyed great popularity at different times and in different countries long after the coming of Christianity, have now dwindled. The significance of the journey of the Magi, however, is imperishable. It has seldom been more vividly evoked than in the childhood memories of the Provençal writer, Frédéric Mistral (1830–1914):

> On the eve of the Feast of the Epiphany it was the custom of all the children of our countryside to go forth to meet the three kings, the wise men from the East, who with their camels and attendants and all their suite came in procession to Maillane there to adore the Holy Child.
>
> One such occasion I well remember. With hearts beating in joyful excitement, eyes full of visions, we sallied forth on the road to Arles, a numerous company of shock-headed urchins and blonde-headed maidens with little hoods and sabots, bearing our offerings of cakes for the kings, dried figs for their pages, and hay for the camels. . . .
>
> The daylight waned. The bell-tower of Maillane disappeared behind the trees, the tall dark pointed cypresses and the wide barren plain stretched away into the dim distance. We strained our eyes as far as they could see, but in vain. . . .
>
> Then we met a shepherd, his cloak wrapped tightly around him, returning from tending his sheep. He asked whither we were bound so late in the day. We inquired anxiously had he seen the kings, and were they still a long way off. Oh, the joy when he replied that he had passed the kings not so very long since—soon we should meet them. Off we set running with all speed, running to meet the kings and present our cakes and handfuls of hay.
>
> Then, just as the sun disappeared behind a great dark cloud and the bravest among us began to flag—suddenly, behold them in sight!
>
> A joyful shout rang from every throat as the magnificence of the royal pageant dazzled our sight. A flash of splendour and gorgeous colour shone in the rays of the setting sun, while the blazing torches showed the gleams of gold on crowns set with rubies and precious stones. The kings! The kings! See their crowns! See their mantles—their flags, and the procession of camels and horses which are coming.
>
> We stood there entranced. But instead of approaching us little by little the glory and the splendour of the vision seemed to melt away before our eyes with the sinking sun, extinguished in the shadows. Crestfallen we stood there, gaping to find ourselves alone on the darkening highway.

Which way did the kings go? They passed behind the mountain.

The white owl hooted. Fear seized us, and huddling together we turned homewards, munching the cakes and figs we had brought for the kings. Our mothers greeted us with, 'Well, did you see them?' Sadly we answered, 'Only afar—they passed behind the mountain.'

'But which road did you take?'

'The road to Arles.'

'Oh, poor lambs—but the kings never come by that road. They come from the East—you should have taken the Roman road. Ah dear, what a pity, you should have seen them enter Maillane. It was a beautiful sight, with their tambours and trumpets, the pages and the camels—it was a show! Now they are gone to the church to offer their adoration. After supper you shall go and see them!'

We supped with speed, I at my grandmother's, and then we ran to the church. It was crowded, and, as we entered, the voices of all the people, accompanied by the organ, burst forth into the superbly majestic Christmas hymn:

> *This morn I met the train*
> *Of the three great kings of the East;*
> *This morn I met the train*
> *Of the kings on the wide high road.*

We children, fascinated, threaded our way between the women, till we reached the Chapel of the Nativity. There, suspended above the altar, was the beautiful star, and bowing the knee in adoration before the Holy Child we beheld at last the three kings: Gaspard, with his crimson mantle, offering a casket of gold; Melchior, arrayed in yellow, bearing in his hands a gift of incense; and Balthazar, with his cloak of blue, presenting a vase of the sadly prophetic myrrh. How we admired the finely dressed pages who upheld the king's flowing mantles, and the great humped camels whose heads rose high above the sacred ass and ox; also the Holy Virgin and St Joseph besides all the wonderful background, a little mountain in painted paper with shepherds and shepherdesses bringing hearth-cakes, baskets of eggs, swaddling clothes, the miller with a sack of corn, the old woman spinning, the knife-grinder at his wheel, the astonished innkeeper at his window, in short, all the traditional crowd who figure in the Nativity, and, above and beyond all, the Moorish king.

16

The Twelfth Day

Behold, there came wise men from the east to Jerusalem, saying, 'Where is he that is born King of the Jews? For we have seen his star in the east, and are come to worship him.'

When Herod the King had heard these things, he was troubled, and all Jerusalem with him. And when he had gathered all the chief priests and scribes of the people together, he demanded of them where Christ should be born. And they said unto him, 'In Bethlehem of Judaea: for thus it is written by the prophet: And thou Bethlehem, in the land of Juda, are not the least among the princes of Juda: for out of thee shall come a governor, that shall rule my people Israel.'

Then Herod, when he had privily called the wise men, inquired of them diligently what time the star appeared. And he sent them to Bethlehem, and said, 'Go and search diligently for the young child; and when ye have found him, bring me word again, that I may come and worship him also.'

When they had heard the king, they departed; and, lo, the star, which they saw in the east, went before them, till it came and stood over where the young child was. When they saw the star, they rejoiced with exceeding great joy.

And when they were come into the house, they saw the young child with Mary his mother, and fell down, and worshipped him: and when they had opened their treasures, they presented unto him gifts; gold, and frankincense, and myrrh.

Thus, in the words of the Gospel according to St Matthew, is described the Epiphany, or the bodily manifestation of Christ to the Magi. The journey and its climax have been pictured and described in a near infinity of manners—none more pungently, perhaps, than that of T. S. Eliot:

THE JOURNEY OF THE MAGI

A cold coming we had of it,
Just the worst time of the year
For a journey, and such a long journey:
The ways deep and the weather sharp,
The very dead of winter.
And the camels galled, sore-footed, refractory,
Lying down in the melting snow.
There were times we regretted
The summer palaces on slopes, the terraces,
And the silken girls bringing sherbet.
Then the camel men cursing and grumbling
And running away, and wanting their liquor and women,
And the night-fires going out, and the lack of shelters,
And the cities hostile and the towns unfriendly
And the villages dirty and charging high prices:
A hard time we had of it.
At the end we preferred to travel all night,
Sleeping in snatches,
With the voices singing in our ears, saying
That this was all folly.

Then at dawn we came down to a temperate valley,
Wet, below the snow line, smelling of vegetation;
With a running stream and a water-mill beating the darkness,
And three trees on the low sky,
And an old white horse galloped away in the meadow.
Then we came to a tavern with vine-leaves over the lintel,
Six hands at an open door dicing for pieces of silver,
And feet kicking the empty wine-skins.
But there was no information, and so we continued
And arrived at evening, not a moment too soon
Finding the place; it was (you may say) satisfactory.

All this was a long time ago, I remember,
And I would do it again, but set down
This set down
This: were we led all that way for
Birth or Death? There was a Birth, certainly,
We had evidence and no doubt. I had seen birth and death,
But had thought they were different; this Birth was
Hard and bitter agony for us, like Death, our death.

We returned to our places, these Kingdoms,
But no longer at ease here, in the old dispensation,
With an alien people clutching their gods.
I should be glad of another death.

In the eastern Church the Birth of the Redeemer was long celebrated on Epiphany, which was regarded by it as the first manifestation of Christ's glory. Possibly as early as the second century a Christian sect had kept this day as the feast of the Baptism, and possibly of the Nativity also; this very early celebration may well have been an adaptation of a heathen rite.

Today the Armenian Church still disregards 25 December and celebrates the Nativity with the Epiphany. In the Eastern Orthodox Church the Epiphany remains an important festival, no longer celebrating the Nativity but the Baptism of Christ. In the West, of course, 6 January commemorates only the Adoration of the Magi—a subject which has always had a profound appeal for the great painters, who repeatedly delighted in the contrast between poverty and riches, between humility and the splendour adoring it.

Who were these Kings, these Wise Men of the East? The question has perplexed many thinkers. Sir Thomas Browne, in *Pseudodoxia Epidemica, or Enquiries into Vulgar and Common Errors* (1646), tells us:

A common conceit there is of the three Kings of Collein,* conceived to be the wise men that travelled unto our Saviour by direction of the Star, Wherein (omitting the large Discourses of Baronius, Pineda, and Montacutius) that they might be Kings, beside the Ancient Tradition and Authority of many Fathers, the Scripture also implieth: The Gentiles shall come to thy light, and Kings to the brightness of thy rising. The Kings of Thaisis and the Isles, the Kings of Arabia and Saba shall offer gifts; which places most Christians and many Rabbins interpret of the Messiah. Not that they are to be conceived potent Monarchs or mighty Kings; but Toparks, Kings of Cities or narrow Territories; such

* Cologne: in 1164 the Emperor Barbarossa presented the relics of the Kings to that city, where they are housed in a highly ornamental casket in the Chapel of the Three Magi in the cathedral.

The Three Magi. Part of the lower mosaic frieze in the nave of St Appollinaire Nuovo, Ravenna. Sixth century.

The Adoration of the Magi. Walrus ivory, probably from an altar
frontal or retable. German, Cologne, c. 1140. *Victoria and Albert
Museum.*

as were the Kings of Sodam and Gomorrah, the Kings of Jericho and Ai, and such as some conceive the Friends of Job to have been.

But although we grant they were Kings, yet we cannot be assured they were three. For the Scriptures make no mention of any number; and the number of their presents, Gold, Myrrhe, and Frankincense, concludeth not the number of their persons; for these were the commodities of their Country, and such as probably the Queen of Sheba in one person had brought before unto Solomon. . . . And therefore their number being uncertain, what credit is to be given unto their names, Gasper, Melchior, Balthazar, what to the charm thereof against the falling sickness, or what unto their habits, complexions, and corporal accidents, we must rely on their uncertain story, and received pourtraits of Collein.

The sceptical Sir Thomas was in a minority when he cast doubts on the precise number of the Magi, for most ancient authors agreed that it was three. Other details varied; some, for instance, said their names were Galgalath, Magalath, and Tharath. Yet generally—and according to our own Anglo-Saxon chronicles—their names, 'habits, complexions, and corporal accidents' were these:

Melchior, an old man, with grey hair and long beard, brought gold in acknowledgment of the Saviour's sovereignty. Caspar, young and beardless, offered frankincense in recognition of the Holy Child's divinity. Balthazar, who was dark—as if Moorish—with a long flowing beard, brought myrrh as a tribute to the Saviour's humanity. Some say that they were respectively kings of Nubia and Arabia, Godolic and Saba (Sheba), Tarse and Egypt (or the Isle of Egristula).

There are numerous Epiphany customs. Some of them concern the symbolic offering of gold, frankincense, and myrrh. We read in *The Times* of 7 January 1961:

Yesterday being the Feast of the Epiphany, Holy Communion was celebrated in the Chapel Royal, St James's Palace, when the customary offering of gold, frankincense and myrrh was made on behalf of the Queen by Colonel Sidney FitzGerald and Major-General Frederick Beaumont-Nesbit, Gentlemen Ushers to Her

Majesty. The Bishop of London, Dean of her Majesty's Chapels Royal, officiated and presented the offerings.

Likewise, *The Gentleman's Magazine* of 1756 records that:

His Majesty, attended by the principal officers at Court, heralds, pursuivants at arms, etcetera, went to the Chapel Royal at St James's and offered gold, myrrh and frankincense. In the evening, His Majesty played at hazard, according to annual custom.

When this tradition of royal Twelfth-Day gambling began we do not know. But nearly a century earlier John Evelyn had described how

according to custom, His Majesty Charles II opened the revels of the night by throwing the dice himself in the Privy Chamber, where there was a table set on purpose, and lost his £100. The year before he won £150. The ladies also played very deep. I came away when the Duke of Ormonde had won about £1,000.

This Court custom was not abolished until George III's reign, in 1772. There was even a special officer, the Groom Porter, who was responsible for providing the cards and making the arrangements.

An ancient custom observed in many northern countries in varying forms was one to which we have already referred, the election of the King of the Bean, who has been portrayed in several paintings, especially by Dutch artists. A cake was provided into which a bean and pea were put before baking. The party cut the cake, and he who had the slice with the bean in it was king, she who came upon the pea, queen. If a man by chance drew the pea, he could choose his consort, or a girl finding the bean could choose her king.

The following sequence was described by Herrick in his '*Twelfe night* or King *and* Queen', 1648:

Now, now the mirth comes
With the cake full of plums,
Where Beane's the *King* of the sport here;
Beside, we must know,
The Pea also
Must revell, as *Queene* for the night here.

Begin then to chase,
(This night as ye use)
Who shall for the present delight here,
Be a *King* by the lot,
And who shall not
Be Twelfe-day *Queene* for the night here.

Which knowne, let us make
Joy-sops with the cake;
And let not a man then be seen here,
Who unurg'd will not drinke
To the base from the brink
A health to the King and the Queene here.

Next crowne the bowl full
With gentle lambs-wooll;
Adde sugar, nutmeg and ginger,
With store of ale too;
And thus ye must doe
To make the wassaile a swinger.

Give then to the King
And Queene wassailing;
And though with ale ye be whet here;
Yet part ye from hence,
As free from offence,
As when ye innocent met here.

On Twelfth Night, 1665, Samuel Pepys, after choosing his piece of cake, 'went to my viall, leaving my wife and people up at their sports, which they continued till morning, not coming to bed at all'. On 6 January a year later his diary describes an elaboration of the cake-cutting.

After cards to choose king and queen, and a good cake there was, but no marks found; but I privately found the clove, the mark of the Knave, and privately put it into Captain Cocke's piece, which made some mirth, because of his lately being known by his buying clove and mace of the East India prizes. At night, home to my lodging. It being Twelfth Night, they had got the fiddler, and mighty merry they were; and I above, came not to them, leaving them dancing and choosing King and Queen.

When James Boswell was in London during 1763 he recorded that on 6 January, being Twelfth Day, a great deal of jollity went on in England 'at the eating of the Twelfth Cake all sugared over'.

It is remarkable how quickly the Twelfth Night celebrations have vanished. Only just over a hundred years ago Leigh Hunt wrote:

> Christmas goes out in fine style—with Twelfth Night. It is a finish worthy of the time. Christmas Day was the morning of the season; New Year's Day the middle of it or noon; Twelfth Night is the night, brilliant with the innumerable planets of Twelfth-cakes.
>
> The whole island keeps court; nay, all Christendom. All the world are kings and queens. Everbody is somebody else; and learns at once to laugh at, and to tolerate, characters different from his own by enacting them. Cakes, characters, forfeits, lights, theatres, merry rooms, little holiday-faces, and, last but not least, the painted sugar on the cakes, so bad to eat but so fine to look at, useful because it is perfectly useless except for a sight and a moral —all conspires to throw a giddy splendour over the last night of the season . . .

Sixteen years later the antiquarian William Sandys said of Twelfth Night that 'in our time it is probably the most popular day throughout the Christmas, thanks to the Twelfth Cake and other amusements'. Well into the latter part of the century the 'epiphany' was to be seen in pastry-cooks' shops, which were illumined to show cakes of every sort, but particularly masterpieces in icing sugar. Urchins regarded this display as a sort of April Fool's night and surreptitiously tacked the tails of the coats of those who were shop-gazing to the window frame. This caper seems to have been taken in good humour by all.

Today the Twelfth Night cake tradition lingers on only at the Theatre Royal, Drury Lane, where attendants wearing eighteenth-century livery and wigs carry a cake into the Green Room. When Robert Baddeley—chef turned actor—died in 1794 he left £100 in Three-per-cent Funds, the interest to be used for making and baking a cake to be eaten every Twelfth Night by the company of His Majesty's Comedians appearing at the theatre, so that his memory should be kept fresh.

Perhaps the Christmas cake of today is the Twelfth Night cake of former years, transferred to a more convenient date. But no trace remains of another Twelfth Night oddity—the Twelfth Night characters. Readers of Thackeray will remember that they were referred to in his fire-side pantomime, *The Rose and the Ring*, in 1854, as 'those funny painted pictures of the King, the Queen, the Lover, the Lady, the Dandy, the Captain, and so on—with which our young are wont to recreate

Engraving from William Hone's *Everyday Book*, 1826

themselves at this time of the year'. From contemporary magazines one learns that the 'so on' included Captain Blunderbuss, Farmer Mangel-wurzel, the Duchess of Daffodil, Monsieur François Parlez-Vous, Lady Bluestocking, Lord Goldlace, Patrick O'Tater and many, many others.

All that is now forgotten. Twelfth Day has disappeared from our calendar of customs and occasions, so much so that some people now hold Twelfth Night to be the eve of Twelfth Day; in the seventeenth and eighteenth centuries that was certainly not so.

There is another famous confusion, tersely commented upon by

Samuel Pepys on 6 January 1663: 'To the Duke's house, and there saw *Twelfth-Night* acted well, though it be but a silly play, and not relating at all to the name or day.'

There were other odd customs connected with Twelfth Day. Dr Robert Plot in 1680 recorded that within living memory there had been at the Staffordshire village of Abbots Bromley a sport which the people celebrated on Twelfth Day. They called it the hobby-horse dance, from a person who carried the image of a horse between his legs, and in his

Burning the Bush at Brough.
Engraving from William Hone's *Everyday Book*, 1827

hand a bow and arrow, with which he made a snapping noise, keeping time with the music. With this man danced six others, carrying on their shoulders reindeer heads, three painted white and three red, who danced the hays and other country dances. Happily, the Abbots Bromley horn dance, as it is now called, is once again in being, though it is now danced in September and has acquired a connexion with Robin Hood.

A strange mixture of the fire-festival, holly-tree rites, and fight for a 'sacred' object used to take place at Brough in Westmorland. A holly-tree with torches attached to its branches was carried in procession through the town. It was then thrown to the crowd who were divided into two rival factions, each associated with rival inns, and each band struggled to obtain possession of the burning bush.

Almost universally Christmastide celebrations end with the passing of the Twelfth Night. And on that night the decorations must be removed. But some believed that the day for removal was Candlemas—2 February. Robert Herrick belonged to this school of thought. In either case, the urgency was necessary for the reasons that he gave:

> That so the superstitious find
> No one least branch there left behind:
> For look how many leaves there be
> Neglected there (maids trust to me)
> So many Goblins you shall see.

In looking for a modern counterpart we cannot do better than refer to one of W. H. Auden's American poems:

> Well, so that is that. Now we must dismantle the tree,
> Putting the decorations back into their cardboard boxes—
> Some have got broken—and carrying them up to the attic.
> The holly and mistletoe must be taken down and burnt,
> And the children got ready for school. There are enough
> Left-overs to do, warmed up, for the rest of the week—
> Not that we have much appetite, having drunk such a lot,
> Stayed up so late, attempted—quite unsuccessfully—
> To love all our relatives, and in general
> Grossly overestimated our powers. Once again
> As in previous years we have seen the actual Vision and failed
> To do more than entertain it as an agreeable
> Possibility, once again we have sent Him away
> Begging though to remain His disobedient servant,
> The promising child who cannot keep His word for long.

Christmastide is now ended, and the most appropriate ending we can make to this book is to recite that curious rhyme which, almost alone, keeps alive the tradition of the Twelve Days, each with its improbable, if delectable gifts. This song is now deservedly elevated to the rank of a

Christmas carol, and is sung in churches, though it seems to have originated as a thoroughly irreligious parody. What we know for certain is that it was a game played until far into the last century at Twelfth Night parties, before supper and the eating of mince pies and iced cake.

The hosts and guests sat around, and a leader spoke the first verse. The others in turn repeated it. Then the leader said the first and second —again to be repeated. So it went on until all had said all the verses. Those who failed to get them right surrendered a forfeit.

Before we launch into the ditty, using the version published by J. O. Helliwell in 1842, we ought to mention that other versions include a wide variety of gifts, among them a papingo-eye (a peacock), a goose that was grey, goldspinks, an Arabian baboon, five Limerick oysters, and three grey elephants.

> The first day of Christmas, my true love sent to me
> A partridge in a pear-tree.
>
> The second day of Christmas, my true love sent to me
> Two turtle doves and a partridge in a pear-tree.
>
> The third day of Christmas, my true love sent to me
> Three French hens, two turtle doves and
> A partridge in a pear-tree.
>
> The fourth day of Christmas, my true love sent to me
> Four colly birds,* three French hens, two turtle doves and
> A partridge in a pear-tree.
>
> The fifth day of Christmas, my true love sent to me
> Five gold rings, four colly birds, three French hens,
> Two turtle doves, and a partridge in a pear-tree.
>
> The sixth day of Christmas, my true love sent to me
> Six geese a-laying, five gold rings,
> Four colly birds, three French hens,
> Two turtle doves, and a partridge in a pear-tree.
>
> The seventh day of Christmas, my true love sent to me
> Seven swans a-swimming,

* Blackbirds.

Richard Doyle (1823–83). Twelfth Night Characters. Engraving in the *Illustrated London News*.

Pieter Brueghel (1525–69). The Adoration of the Kings. 1564.
National Gallery.

Six geese a-laying, five gold rings,
Four colly birds, three French hens,
Two turtle doves, and a partridge in a pear-tree.

The eighth day of Christmas, my true love sent to me
Eight maids a-milking, seven swans a-swimming,
Six geese a-laying, five gold rings,
Four colly birds, three French hens, two turtle doves, and
A partridge in a pear-tree.

The ninth day of Christmas, my true love sent to me
Nine drummers drumming, eight maids a-milking,
Seven swans a-swimming, six geese a-laying,
Five gold rings, four colly birds, three French hens,
Two turtle doves, and
A partridge in a pear-tree.

The tenth day of Christmas, my true love sent to me
Ten pipers piping, nine drummers drumming,
Eight maids a-milking, seven swans a-swimming,
Six geese a-laying, five gold rings,
Four colly birds, three French hens,
Two turtle doves, and
A partridge in a pear-tree.

The eleventh day of Christmas, my true love sent to me,
Eleven ladies dancing, ten pipers piping,
Nine drummers drumming, eight maids a-milking,
Seven swans a-swimming, six geese a-laying,
Five gold rings, four colly birds,
Three French hens, two turtle doves and
A partridge in a pear-tree.

The twelfth day of Christmas, my true love sent to me
Twelve lords a-leaping, eleven ladies dancing,
Ten pipers piping, nine drummers drumming,
Eight maids a-milking, seven swans a-swimming,
Six geese a-laying, five gold rings,
Four colly birds, three French hens,
Two turtle doves, and
A partridge in a pear-tree.

Index